Instruct

LET AUGMENTED REALITY CHANGE HOW YOU READ A BOOK

With your smartphone, iPad or tablet you can use the **Hasmark AR** app to invoke the augmented reality experience to literally read outside the book.

1. Download the **Hasmark app** from the **Apple App Store** or **Google Play**

2. Open and select the (vue) option

3. Point your lens at the full image with the and enjoy the augmented reality experience.

Go ahead and try it right now with the Hasmark Publishing International logo.

YOUR PAST Can't BREAK YOU

Based on a True Story

ENDORSEMENTS

Seldom have I seen more wisdom packed into a story about a person's life. This page-turning account of one individual's experience turns out to be about all of our lives, because the illuminating realizations this author shares in every single chapter can be applied to every single one of our own stories. This is an especially powerful book for anyone whose story includes a difficult and hurtful past. In six words, Tehminé Grigorian has given us here a read that is exceptionally helpful, deeply insightful, and wonderfully healing.

—**Neale Donald Walsch,**
bestselling author of the *Conversations with God* series

YOUR PAST *Can't* BREAK YOU

TEHMINÉ GRIGORIAN

Hasmark PUBLISHING INTERNATIONAL

Hasmark Publishing
www.hasmarkpublishing.com

Copyright © 2023 Tehminé Grigorian

First Edition

No part of this book may be reproduced or transmitted in any form or by any means, electronic or mechanical, including photocopying, recording or by any information storage and retrieval system, without written permission from the author, except for the inclusion of brief quotations in a review.

Disclaimer

The information in this book, but not limited to text, graphics, images, and other material ("Content") are provided for motivational, educational, and informational purposes only. This book may make available reference to certain information related to areas of life including, without limitation, relationships, health, psychology, and related matters. This book is meant as a source of valuable information for the reader, however, it is not meant as a substitute for direct expert assistance and should not be interpreted as a recommendation for a specific therapy, medical plan, or other course of action. Use of this information does not replace consultations for professional medical advice, diagnosis, or treatment with a qualified and competent therapist, physician, healthcare worker, or other relevant and qualified professionals. Always seek the advice of your physician or other qualified health provider with any questions you may have regarding any medical or psychological condition. In addition, this information may change rapidly and therefore, some of it may be out of date.

Although the publisher and the author have made every effort to ensure that the information in this book was correct at press time and while this publication is designed to provide accurate information in regards to the subject matter covered, the publisher and the author assume no responsibility for errors, inaccuracies, omissions, or any other inconsistencies herein and hereby disclaim any liability to any party for any loss, damage, or disruption caused by errors or omissions, whether such errors or omission result from negligence, accident, or any other causes. The contents within this book are the sole expression and opinion of its author, and not necessarily that of the publisher.

The publisher and author make no guarantees concerning the level of success you may experience by following the advice and strategies contained in this book, and you accept the risk that results will differ for each individual. Further, the testimonials and examples provided in this book show exceptional results, which may not apply to every reader, and are not intended to represent or guarantee that you will achieve the same or similar results. No warranties or guarantees are expressed or implied by the publisher and the author to include any of the content in this volume.

You agree that all risk associated with the use of, or reliance on, any of this information provided in this book directly or indirectly linked to this book solely rests with you. You further agree that the publisher and the author, including their respective agents, shall not be responsible or liable, directly or indirectly, in any way for any loss or damage of any kind incurred as a result of, or in connection with your use of, or reliance on, any such information herein.

Neither the publisher or author shall be liable for any physical, psychological, emotional, financial, or commercial damages, including, but not limited to, special, incidental, consequential or other damages.

Permission should be addressed in writing to Tehminé Grigorian at Tgrigorian@hotmail.fr

Editor: Deanna Novak deanna@thewritejourneys.com
Cover Design: Anne Karklins anne@hasmarkpublishing.com
Interior Layout: Amit Dey amit@hasmarkpublishing.com

ISBN 13: 978-1-77482-206-7
ISBN 10: 1774822067

Content Warning: This book contains references to alcohol consumption, domestic violence, and child abuse.

DEDICATION

I dedicate this entire book to my loving mom. Without her and her story, I wouldn't even be here to write these lines. She is the woman who fought for me and my sister in order to protect us, the woman who stood up each time she was down. The woman who prayed night and day for her two daughters. The woman who didn't eat the last piece of bread so that we could have it. The woman who had sleepless nights and shed tears for us. The woman who sacrificed her life for us.

> To this strong, loving, courageous woman.
> To my mom.
> To my hero.
> To my angel.
> With all my Love.

TABLE OF CONTENTS

Foreword xi
Acknowledgments xiii
Preface xv
Introduction or Prologue xvii

  1. In The Beginning 1
  2. Choices Matter 5
  3. The Innocence of a Child 13
  4. A Matter of Perspective 23
  5. The Importance of Role Models 29
  6. A Sister's Love 37
  7. Finding Light in the Darkness 43
  8. In Pursuit of a New Life 49
  9. Growth and Determination Through Challenges 55
10. Finding Success 65
11. History Will Try to Repeat Itself, But It Doesn't Have To 71
12. Loving and Letting Go 77
13. Willpower and Mindset 85

14. Acceptance and Love................................ 91
15. Forgiveness.. 97
16. Life Experiences and the Possibilities they Uncover.. 101

Epilogue.. 107
The Power of Poetry..................................... 111
About the Author....................................... 117

FOREWORD

You are about to read the story of a person's life. That person is you.

What appears to be the story of a young woman named Tehminé Grigorian, in this riveting account of her experiences in life, turns out to be about all of our lives: because the illuminating realizations this author shares in every single chapter can be applied to every single one of our own stories.

The lives of all of us on this planet contain essentially the same emotional elements—success, failure, happiness, sadness, kindness, abuse, gratitude, grievance, healing, injury, ease, struggle, loyalty, betrayal, etc. There are differences in our experiences, of course, but they seem to me to be matters of degree. More of some, less of another.

Now…if a book about another person's life could produce a ton of immediately usable wisdom, and vivid descriptions of responses that *work* when our own experiences—past or present—are starkly negative, would that be a good reason to reason to read it?

I think, yes. And I am so glad that I did. It confirmed for me the resilience of the human spirit and restored my faith in myself to meet life head-on. I couldn't have asked for more.

Be glad, then, that this book has found its way to you. Or perhaps it's the other way around. Perhaps you found your way to *it,* knowing at some inner level that it would be very valuable for you to have come across this bounty.

This is an especially powerful book for anyone whose life story includes a difficult and hurtful past. It is not easy to overcome deeply injurious experiences. Their after-effects can linger for years (indeed, for decades), and can become major obstacles on one's life path.

Now it's true that one can go into any brick-and-mortar bookstore, or search any online bookseller's website, and find a plethora of Self-Help books that tell us all about how we can deal with the most unwelcome emotional elements that I mentioned earlier. But I must be honest with you. I have found too many of them to be dry, academic recitations, or—even more sad—predictable summaries of formulaic panaceas.

I have seldom seen in such books the kind of self-reflective searing wisdom and striking, on-point situational insight that emerges from the narrative regarding her tumultuous real-life encounters that Tehminé Grigorian offers here.

In six words, she has given us a read that is exceptionally helpful, deeply insightful, and wonderfully healing.

I trust you will agree and will recommend this book to anyone you know whose past has been challenging, yet whose future can be positive and joyous at last, given the tools woven into the storyline here, and the encouragement of one whose difficult Yesterdays have not blocked the creation of wonderful Todays, and the promise of very special Tomorrows.

—Neale Donald Walsch, bestselling author
of the *Conversations with God* series

ACKNOWLEDGMENTS

Thank you to my sister for her presence in my life and for all of her support, always.

Thank you to those who have crossed my path on this incredible journey called life.

Thank you also to those who have allowed me to have growth-inspiring experiences. They have given me opportunities to improve myself and have helped me become who I am today.

And thank you to our Higher Being for your presence in my life and the guidance you provide throughout it.

I gratefully acknowledge author Neale Donald Walsch for providing me with the inspiration that allows me to know who I truly am. You have changed my life forever.

♡ ♡ ♡

PREFACE

Life doesn't always bring us flowers. Personal, professional, health-related, and familial challenges surround us all—sometimes out on the horizon, sometimes right there in front of us. And while we all should know that we cannot control that which is outside us, the fact of the matter is we tend to allow it all in at some point. We tend to believe that those circumstances, those challenges define us and our future. But they don't have the power to do that. In fact, we are the only ones with that kind of power.

It is up to us to raise our awareness and open our hearts and minds to all the possibilities that surround us, rather than focusing on the challenges and circumstances of our pasts. For many of us, that means changing our mindsets from acceptance of our current state to deserving more of everything that makes us happy and gives us peace. With that mindset, feelings of gratitude and worthiness begin to replace lack and worthlessness. But only with awareness and self-love can we begin to make these important shifts.

We all have the capacity to change our mindsets, but for one reason or another, we are the ones who build barriers to do so. Most of the time, we don't even realize that it is our own thoughts, centered in our ego, that are getting in our own way.

It is the ego that dictates whether we act with anger and hatred, and it is the ego that makes us think that it is always someone else's fault. The key is recognizing the ego and its place, but not allowing it to control our lives.

The ego will never bring us happiness, nor will it heal our pain or suffering. It can certainly make us feel good at times, but unfortunately, that feeling is fleeting. True peace and happiness can only ever be found inside us. When we learn to reach within ourselves, we will find it all right there—the love for ourselves that leads to joy, peace, and happiness. Love for others and love for ourselves is what allows us to heal from any kind of trauma we have experienced in our lives, whether as a child or as an adult. This is the key that opens the door to our future—the future that only we have the power to create and mold—no one else. When we listen to the voice of the heart (some people call it intuition or the voice of the divine), it will show us the way to everything we need to create happiness. And when we take control of our thoughts, actions, and choices, we become the masters of our lives.

My hope is that you are able to relate to parts of my story (or of my mother's) in this book, and that this connection will provide you with the strength to overcome the challenges in your own life.

This book is based on a true story.

INTRODUCTION OR PROLOGUE

"**G**o get me a glass of water."

Who knew that such a seemingly simple demand would change the trajectory of my entire life.

"No! I don't want to!" My five-year-old self yelled back to my stepfather in between laughs, as I continued to jump on the bed. I was carefree and giddy with excitement to be with my mom. I didn't get to see her often and was having so much fun.

"Go get me a glass of water, right now!"

"Nooooo!" I said, again through giggles, with the cheery attitude and pure joy that can only be found in a young, innocent child.

But that was about to change. My life was about to change.

Maybe my mom saw the shift in him. (I think she had witnessed it before.)

"I'll go get it," she said.

"No, you won't. I won't allow it."

Before I knew what was happening, he grabbed my arm with one of his hands, stopping me from jumping, and with the other, slapped me in the face. Hard. The force of it knocked me down. And then, the second slap came, and then a third. I felt like a rag doll being tossed carelessly around the room.

Mom tried to stop him, but it didn't work. And then, he turned his rage on her. I was crying and screaming for him to stop, but it only seemed to make him hit her harder. The commotion woke everyone in the house. I remember hearing someone come in the room. I thought—*Oh good! Someone is going to help us!*

But help wasn't coming at all. I remember that my step-grandmother pushed my mother out of the room—not to help her, as I originally thought, but to get her out of the way from helping me. Mom said she forced her out and shut the door behind them. Then my step-grandmother stood outside to make sure no one else could get in, so my 'dad' could teach me a lesson in manners. He was slapping me across my face inside the room, while my step-grandmother was telling my mom just outside, "She is not educated, she has to learn."

Mom was so relieved when my step-uncle soon came running toward the door, pushed his mother out of his way, and came into the room. Grabbing me quickly from my stepfather's hold, he took me to his sister, my step-aunt. She cried when she saw my face, took me in her arms lovingly, and put me in her bed. She cuddled me protectively all night, brushing the hair out of my face and whispering words of comfort to try to get me to sleep. I couldn't sleep though. Despite her loving arms around me, I had no idea what just happened or how my mom was doing. But I also began to think my step-uncle and step-aunt were my heroes. After all, we all need a hero once in a while … especially when we're just five years old.

CHAPTER 1

IN THE BEGINNING

Armenia is a small country with a beautiful, rocky terrain that meets lush green landscapes. It is an old Christian country. In fact, Armenia was the first country in the world to accept Christianity as their official religion in 301 A.D. The origin of the Armenian language comes from Indo-European. From anywhere in the country, you will breathe fresh, clean air, drink tasty, cold spring water, hear calming sounds of nature, and gaze upon beautiful trees that produce many kinds of fruits. The apricot and pomegranate (the symbolic fruit of Armenia) trees, the language, the food, and the arts all contribute to a culture that leaves the door open for everyone, whispering "Welcome" to all who want to experience its beauty.

Armenia is a country very rich in this friendly culture. People are born with hospitality and openness—the desire to help others in need, even strangers, is simply pulsing in their blood. These are some of the values of most Armenians. It is a country that is evolving, along with its people, but its incredible beauty and lofty ideals and values will never change.

Like every other country, people have different lifestyles, different experiences, and different educational backgrounds. There are those who know their way and stay true to their values, and those who need more support and guidance throughout their lives. There are places that are warm and friendly, and others that are colder and more hostile. Armenia is no exception.

This is where Mom's story (and of course, my own) begins.

I was born in Yerevan, Armenia, and was fortunate enough to grow up in Goshavank, a small village with a population of only 1,500 people, where my grandparents owned what had once been a vacation home. As you can probably imagine about a village that small, everyone knew each other, and many people were related. You couldn't hide from anyone there. It was the type of place where everyone knew about each other's life—where they were and what they were doing, likely even what they ate for breakfast. And then, of course, they'd give you their opinion about it all. That's just small village living—it's like one big family. Although it sounds silly and intrusive, everyone meant well and were loving and helpful toward each other. If one neighbor needed help, the whole village would turn up to offer their assistance, either with food, wood for heating, or with planting and farming. I am grateful for this part of my upbringing.

Back then, Armenia was a part of the USSR. At that time, most of the population had jobs that paid a decent wage, so people could afford homes. That all changed when Armenia took its independence in 1991. Everything was different then. We had water and electricity for only short periods of time. I can remember that when the electricity came on, the neighbors would open their front doors or stick their heads outside windows to yell that it was back on. During those times that we had electricity, everyone took advantage of the opportunity to get things done—filling buckets with water, cooking, washing dishes, or doing laundry. We even had time to watch a bit of television.

Some of my fondest memories are of the times we were all gathered together in the evening under the light of the oil lamp, next to a warm, glowing fire that cast dancing shadows on the walls. The adults were chatting about their day, telling stories of their lives, perhaps playing cards or bingo. The kids were doing their studies by the soft glow of candlelight. We had many laughs in those moments that will be etched in my memories forever. Despite all the difficulties we had, we were happy. It is true that we may not have always had enough to eat, but we had more than enough love in our hearts to make up for it. This is what we called happiness—the happiness that can only be found in the cozy comfort of loved ones.

Mom recalls that in her early years, she was a happy girl living her lighthearted days with her parents and older sister and brother in the capital city (the house in the village was more of a vacation home back then). The neighbors and family friends knew her as kind and generous, as well as the girl who made the most delicious desserts. She remembers that they lived well. Her father, my grandfather, consistently worked and was financially stable. People even referred to him as the 'Millionaire Vladimir' (although he was far from a millionaire). It was his generosity that made people think that he was rich. And it was his generosity that actually made us rich—in values, love, and kindness.

My mom tells me that the food was often overflowing, and they always had people at the house for dinner. My grandfather would even bring people in from the street to have a hot meal. I actually remember him saying to my grandmother, "Madam, when you are making soup, always add an extra cup of water and a bit more of everything. Maybe someone will come unexpectedly, and that person is a guest sent by God." I also remember that we always set one more place at the table in case that unexpected person did show up. Then, we would have a plate for them, and they would feel that they were welcome. This is what I mean by the warmth and hospitality of Armenians.

Mom still remembers and tells us with a big smile that there was always music, chanting, and dancing while she was growing up. It was a happy childhood. And she never saw my grandfather be violent toward my grandmother, either verbally or physically. Of course, they had an occasional disagreement, like all couples do, but there was never any violence. She remembers laughter and love, innocence and free will. She remembers being a carefree young girl, who loved and was loved.

This was Mom's life before she married my father. She went from a life of joy, happiness, and peace to a life of hell.

CHAPTER 2

CHOICES MATTER

Mom was twenty-two years old when she chose to marry my father. She described him as a tall, handsome man with beautiful green eyes. (I look like my father, right down to those piercing green eyes.) He was a quiet man—that is, when he was sober. But he was an alcoholic, so times of sobriety were few and far between. Mom said she hadn't noticed the problem with alcohol until after they were married. He had been able to hide the symptoms very well up until then. She now realizes what a huge red flag it was when he came home drunk the day after they were married. Yet isn't hindsight always 20/20?

According to Mom, the verbal and physical abuse started not long after that day, and continued even while she was pregnant with me. But, as victims often do, she would defend him constantly, making excuses for his horrendous behavior. She said she repeatedly insisted that he was a sweet and wonderful man without the alcohol, but when he drank, he completely changed into someone else. At the time, she still held onto hope that the man she fell in love with would be the man she would live her life with. She didn't realize how much this "other" man would change everything, but she soon would.

Mom told me that one night, when I was about six months old, he came home with some friends, and of course, even more alcohol. The problem on this specific night (compared to all the others), according to Mom, was that his friends were teenagers. When she saw the kids drinking, she asked my father what he was doing with these kids and why he was allowing them to drink. He didn't answer her. So, she told the young men to stop drinking and go home. All the while, she knew she would pay the price later for going against him, but she wanted the kids to go home to their parents. It was all to no avail. They ignored her and continued drinking. By the time they finally went home, my father was very drunk.

Mom said that when he walked into the kitchen, she knew what was coming and tried to brace herself. He walked directly to her, looked her in the eye, and spit in her face. Then, she told me that he kicked her and started beating her, screaming, "Why did you tell me 'Don't drink' in front of my friends?" He then grabbed the large bread knife from the counter and tried to stab her. Somehow, Mom escaped from his hands and caught him off guard. She used his surprise to her advantage and forcefully grabbed him by the front of his shirt, pushing him against the wall and quickly grabbing the knife from his hand. He was shocked that she would react that way—she never had before. After his sudden shock subsided, he ran into the living room, where his mother was holding me. Mom said he grabbed me (a six-month-old baby) and used me as a shield to protect himself from my mother.

He screamed at her, holding me out in front of him in between the two of them, "Now go ahead and stab me, stab me now!"

Mom was so upset, she said she couldn't help but start shaking as she tried to negotiate with him, saying, "Put that child down, give me that child now!"

She remembers even trying to play a submissive role, telling him she was sorry, and she was wrong, just to try to take me from his hands. But it was backfiring, and he was getting angrier by the minute. Somehow, Mom slowly reached the door. She opened it and ran out with the knife still in her hands, desperate to get help. She remembers running all the way to the street to try to stop a car that could drive her to her brother's home or to the police station.

Of course, you can't get a car to stop for you in the middle of the night with a knife in your hands. So, she continued on foot until she found a gas station, where some taxies were parked. She was still without shoes (they had fallen off while she was running) and did not realize that she still had the knife in her hand. Everyone was looking at her and laughing. *What was this crazy woman doing in the street at 1:00 a.m. without shoes and with a knife?*

She tried asking the taxi drivers to take her downtown, but no one was answering her. They continued to ridicule her. Then she raised her voice and screamed, "What are you laughing at? Are you waiting for someone to be killed? I didn't do anything! I just ran away from a drunk husband! Please! I need to go downtown or to the police station."

One man took pity on her and said, "Come on, I will drive you to the police station."

He put Mom in his taxi quietly. When they got there, the first police officer she saw calmly took the knife from her hand.

Mom said she told him that no one was hurt and began to explain the situation. She was crying hysterically by this point.

"My child is with him, please go get her!"

She also told him that she left to get help because she knew he would never hurt me. She was the target of his wrath when he was drunk. When the police officer went to our home, they didn't find him there. However, they did see that his mother (my grandmother) was taking care of me and that I was safe. They also informed my mom that with everything that she had told them, he could be charged and go to jail. They told her it was her *choice*.

"You fill out the papers and then he goes to jail."

Mom thought for a moment and told them she couldn't do it. After all of that, she still took pity on him. They told her that there were only two choices here—either jail or a hospital for alcohol addiction. Of course, she chose the hospital. They located him, brought him in to the police station, and then drove him directly to the hospital. Mom was so happy that he would finally get some help. She hoped that he would come back sober and that they could live the fairytale life she had always thought they would have.

Within only four days, he also made a *choice*. He ran away from the hospital. And for a little while, he surprised Mom. He didn't go out and drink—for one entire week. He stayed home and was pleasant and even sweet to Mom and to me. She thought he had changed, and everything was going to be okay. However, after that first week, he went out and came home drunk once again.

Mom asked him, "Why did you drink again?"

She remembers him saying, "I couldn't not drink. My friends said that those who can't drink are not men."

So, to prove to them that he was a man, he drank. Mom said she was so disappointed, realizing that her heart was breaking all over again. She continued to deal with both his daily bouts of extreme violence and her broken heart for three long years—three years that felt like a lifetime—three years of enduring violence at the hands of someone she loved, all while caring for her young daughter. And then, she made a new *choice*—she chose to leave.

One day, they planned to go visit my grandparents and she pleaded with my father, "Please don't drink over there, not in front of everyone. There will be a lot of people. If you want to drink, do it at home."

According to Mom, he became angry and yelled, "Fuck everything! I don't need you, and I don't need your family. Do you think it's only you? There are a lot of women that would love to have me."

That's when it clicked, so to speak. Mom said, "Oh, okay. I am not the only one. Good. Now, let's see, what do you have in this house? Take it with you and never come back."

She turned around and grabbed everything she could that belonged to my father, put it all in a bag, and said, "Now go, and be happy."

Stunned, he grabbed his bag and walked out the door.

After he left, Mom said she didn't cry. She celebrated! She made a cake, got a bottle of champagne, and went to her aunt's home. She told her, "We have to celebrate! He left, and thanks be to God!"

The ironic thing is that Mom ended up being a "marriage fixer" for him later. When he eventually remarried and there was trouble (which, of course, there was), he would come to see Mom and ask her to call his new wife to encourage her to take him back. Another time, he came to Mom and said, "Please call her again."

Mom told her, "Take him back! If not, I am taking him back."

Her strategy worked. She created enough jealousy that the other woman took him back. Mom was ready every time and knew what card to play and would play when she needed to.

But what changed everything for us was her *choice*.

Choices

Mom first had made a choice to not send him to jail. And then he had made his own choice to live a life with alcohol. Mom made a choice to stay, but then another choice later to leave.

Each one of us, alone, is responsible for the choices we make. Our present reality is the direct result of all of our past choices. And the choices we make today are creating our future. But it's not just that there are good or bad choices. It's the fact that every single choice has consequences. Consciously, we know that, but it is easy to forget in the moment. And we often make subconscious decisions without thinking them through.

The key is in the awareness of the results stemming from the choices we make. If you don't like the results, you can choose (there's that word again) to make changes. We can change our thoughts, our habits, our behaviors, and the perspective or meaning we give to them all. The good news? That means it is never too late to change the direction of our lives. It means that we can always choose to change our path, regardless of what it looked like before.

The fact is we are making choices every single day. We decide what to wear, what to eat, where to go, and what to do. Without choices, we would never move forward at all. More importantly, if we don't make our own choices, someone or something else will likely do so for us.

But make no mistake, choosing not to choose is a choice. Most of the time, when we hesitate to make a choice, it is often based in the fear of the unknown or of making a mistake. It is from that place of fear that we prefer to stay in the comfort of the shadows of what we know, rather than go to an unknown future. Even if we choose to stay in a given situation, there is no way to know what that decision will entail or the effect it will have on us. Every decision has consequences—positive, negative, or simply neutral.

When you suffer abuse of any kind, the fear that holds you back is even more powerful. In my mother's case, she finally found the courage to say no to her abusive husband—three long years after the abuse began. To many, it may seem too long, but an abuse victim's state of mind is altered as a result of physical, mental, and emotional abuse. On top of that, they have every reason to be fearful. She needed that time to face her fear and find the courage to take her life into her own hands. Ultimately, she made the choice to leave him and no longer accept that domestic violence would be her life. That was the best life-changing decision she could have made. Unfortunately, my father also made his decision to continue drinking into a downward spiral that became his life. But again, they each made a choice that they would have to live with.

CHAPTER 3

THE INNOCENCE OF A CHILD

Mom has told me that even as a baby, I would never go to my biological father. She says I would cry and kick and scream each time he held me. And even from a very young age, I would never call him 'Daddy.' Each time I was asked to call him that, I refused. And anytime he would try to hug me, I would cry more. Mom says he would beat her for that too. He would yell at her, demanding to know, "What did you do that this child doesn't want to come to me?" He didn't understand that it had nothing to do with Mom, but everything to do with him. I could feel his hostility even then.

What most people don't realize is that children have an innate sense of those around them and an extremely strong instinct because they haven't been programmed or trained to doubt those feelings yet. Even though babies and children are small physically, their innocence and capacity to read negative energy and avoid it is immense. Mom recalls that while she was pregnant with me, she was continuously abused. And I am sure I felt all of it in my mother's womb. In fact, it has been scientifically proven that even in the womb, fetuses can feel pain in the emotions of the mother.

Mom started dating again and then got married and introduced me to her new husband. To her surprise and delight, she said I immediately ran to him and called him 'Dad' without any prompting. She hadn't even had time to explain to me or ask me to consider him as a father. I went to him with the innocent heart of a child. Maybe I thought I would have a father who would actually be nice and not hurt us. Maybe I felt this father would take care of us, and we would finally have a "normal," stable family. And despite the horrible times with him, I still refer to him as 'Dad' or 'Daddy' to this day.

In her new married household, my mom lived with her new husband and also her mother-in-law, father-in-law, her brother- and sister-in-law and their children, and her other sister-in-law. Somehow, they all lived together in a two-bedroom apartment. And sadly, it wasn't long before Mom realized that her new married life wouldn't be terribly different from her old one. When the abuse began, she decided I would be safer with my grandparents, which is where I stayed until I was fifteen years old.

I would visit my mom and stepfather in the summer, so happy and excited to see them. I loved being with my grandparents, but I missed my mom so much. And on one of those trips, when I was just five years old, my stepfather beat me for not getting him a glass of water. The next morning, I was still in shock.

I was sitting on the sofa when my great-aunt, who had lived next door, walked into the house. She was elderly and extremely kind. She saw my face, swollen and bruised, with red handprints still all over it. As she moved closer, she could see that both of my eyes had been blackened and were swollen shut. I could barely see her, but I heard her. She said to my step-grandmother, "Shame on you! What did you all do to this child? I hope God will punish you for what you did to her. Oh my God, I can't stay here and watch what you have done to this child."

She was a lovely auntie. She had always been nice to me and my mom and always took care of me when I was visiting—that day was no exception. She asked me if I would like to come over to her house. I stood up tentatively, not sure what I was supposed to do or how I should act. Seeing my hesitation, she grabbed my hand and guided me out the door. She sat me on a chair in her warm, inviting kitchen and asked what I wanted to eat, telling me she would fix me anything I wanted. Her daughter lived next door and came over as well. She hugged me tighter than usual. We were very close. They were nice to me. They had welcomed me as part of the family and never treated me any different than their own kids. I still love them dearly.

While I was there, my mom was calling my grandparents to come pick me up early. The village we lived in wasn't nearby, so it took three days before they got to me. During those few days, I stayed within the protection of my mom's arms as much as possible and tried to avoid my stepfather. The internal innocence of a young child will overshadow any physical trauma … at least for a while, anyway. The day they arrived, I was playing outside with neighborhood children, almost as if nothing had ever happened. Even with black eyes and a swollen face, I was having fun. Children are, after all, incredibly resilient.

When I saw my grandma coming toward me, I ran into her arms. Wherever we were, whatever time it was, her arms were my home. I was so happy to see her, but she did not mirror that emotion. Of course, she was happy to have me safe with her, but she was horrified when she saw my small battered and bruised face. She didn't say a word to my mom and told my grandfather we were leaving immediately.

I didn't see my mom for a long time after that, and I missed her so much. But I was also so worried about her. I kept thinking about how he hit her and how somehow, I knew it wasn't the first or the last time. Unfortunately, history had repeated itself. This obviously wasn't the first time she had felt the heavy hand of someone whom she was supposed to trust the most.

One of the next times I saw them was nearly three years later, when my mom, stepfather, and new baby sister came to the village for a vacation and stayed with us at our home. The rest of the family had gone to work in the potato fields, while my stepfather, who I still called 'Daddy,' helped me with my homework after school. He was a strict disciplinarian, and of course, a violent man. I wasn't allowed out of the chair until I had finished my work and knew my math times tables perfectly.

If he found one small mistake, or one number that wasn't written nicely, he would slap my hands—then he would make a habit of going too far. I was in the process of learning the three times tables in multiplication. Mathematics was not necessarily my best subject, especially when I was put on the spot and expected to answer instantly. My stepfather put me in a room and closed the door, telling me I couldn't come out until I knew the answers. He would give me an hour and then call me out and ask what the answer was to 3 x 3. That was easy. I said, "3 x 3 = 9." I feared that if I gave any wrong answers, he would hit me in the face again. For an eight-year-old, when I was alone in the room, it seemed to me that I knew the answers, but once I was in front of him, I couldn't remember. He intimidated me, of course. The next question was, "What is 3 x 4?" I couldn't answer that, so I just stared at him, looking into his face, watching for any sign of rage—I knew this wasn't going to end well. I tried not to show fear and stay strong.

Silently, I prayed to God to please shield me from his wrath. He again repeated, "What is 3 x 4?"

I didn't comprehend what he was saying, as I was busy praying. He said, "Okay, 3 x 7?"

I said a number that was not 21 and what I feared most didn't take long to manifest. He slapped my face with his big heavy hands. He yelled out again, "3 x 7!"

I started to cry, and he said, "Don't cry or you will get another one."

I tried hard to stay strong because I knew another slap or worse would be coming.

At that point, panic set in—I knew that I would get it either way. He then put me in the room again and said, "Until you know it, you are not going to get out."

An hour later he'd come back, and it was the same scenario. He didn't stop slapping me. And so, it went on all afternoon. I was crying in the silence of the room, while praying that it would all be over as soon as my mom and grandparents got home. I did not understand why he would react toward me with such violence.

I was born into a culture of abuse, even though I didn't live with them full-time and only saw them once or twice a year. It began even while my mother was still pregnant with me. She thought that once she divorced my father, none of us would have to live with that kind of domestic violence again. Sadly, she was mistaken. But that was only one part of my life.

In my grandparents' home, there was never any violence whatsoever. My grandfather and uncle were kind and gentle—never violent with anyone. However, I continued to witness all kinds of domestic violence outside our four walls. I remember we had neighbors who tried to educate their children through violence. The fathers beat their children every single day. When asked why, they would respond that they wanted to educate them, so they would become good people. This made no sense and still doesn't, of course. But when you look at it from their perspective, they actually thought they were doing a *good* thing. They were trying to teach their children right from wrong. To them, being strict through violence meant that they were loving their children.

I have also since learned that in some families, male children are not taught how to give love and respect to the women and girls in their lives. Some parents in Armenia give their children the impression that males have absolute authority and that boys should assert that authority early. They are often as young as two or three years old, and it becomes "fun" for them to hit a girl. I have even seen some parents encourage it as a game and think it's funny. Somehow, these parents don't realize that by telling them it is okay to hit a girl, they are planting the seeds of violence in the young child's mind.

Unfortunately, many women in certain countries and cultures may think this behavior is acceptable, and even if they don't, they know that if they object, a slap is coming, and then another, and by the third, it's become a punch. So, they make excuses for these men, rationalizing that their actions are justified.

For many years, I'd heard women in the neighborhood take the blame for being beaten, saying that it was their own fault, that they should have listened to them, or that it was because he was drunk. Sometimes, even when they have no excuses to give, they simply don't have any place to go. They are also often told that it is the way it is, they are married, so they simply must stay with their husband.

I remember one neighbor, in particular, whose husband was very violent and beat her frequently. She would often come over and ask my grandmother if I could sleep at her house with their children. She thought that if her husband saw another child there, he might not dare to beat her. She was wrong—my presence didn't stop him. I thought that although I was a child myself, I was still older than the rest of the children, so I tried to shelter them in my arms on those horrible nights that felt like time had stopped.

One night when I was about ten years old, it got really scary. It was around 2:00 a.m. when her husband came home drunk. We were all sleeping, and I remember waking up to yelling and furniture crashing to the floor. Then I saw my neighbor getting violently beaten by her husband. Their newborn baby and the other kids were awake, and everyone was crying, including me. I was so scared that I opened the door and ran out of the house in the middle of the night. In tears, I ran to the home of another family member nearby, pounding on the door, pleading with them to open it. They were frightened to hear a child crying and yelling at the door. When they opened it, I begged them to take me home to my grandmother.

They didn't have a car, so it took the woman about twenty minutes to walk me home around 3:00 a.m. Grandma said she was going to talk to him the next morning, and I was so relieved when she said she would not send me there anymore. But for that night, I was safe with my grandmother and I slept peacefully. As an innocent child, we don't perceive things in the same way an adult does. In the morning, I awoke as if nothing had happened. I went outside to play, blissfully unaware of the extent of the damage being done in that household.

Innocence can only protect a child for so long

I was surrounded by domestic violence and abuse—of all types—and it made a huge impact on how I felt about myself and the world around me, as it does for so many children living in a culture of abuse. By the time the child is an adult, these negative feelings and emotions can destroy their self-esteem and confidence, leaving them with feelings of inadequacy, worthlessness, and most importantly, the feeling of being unlovable. Most of the time, these are the feelings that destabilize our lives.

The parents who think violence is needed to educate are completely wrong. Violence teaches nothing but disrespect and a lack of human empathy. It never fixes problems, but instead only adds to them. Yet, in time, and with new perspective, we can learn to understand, forgive, appreciate, and love this person's good qualities. We can do this as we live our lives separately and peacefully. This is the way to find the solution.

Over many trips to Armenia from the time I was a child, I have noticed that the culture is evolving. Now, when I am visiting, I can see the differences. Kids are treated with more respect than when I was growing up. There is even a holiday dedicated to children on the 1st of June of each year, called Children's Day. I can also see more respect, more open minds, and more friendships between men and women. This does not mean domestic violence or child abuse no longer exist. As we all know, unfortunately, abuse does not know geographical limits. But it does mean that I love seeing that these relationships have grown with mutual respect and adoration. It makes me proud that my beautiful Armenia is evolving in such a strong, impactful way. These important relationships mirror more closely the extraordinary nature of the country—where the beauty of the land is reflected in the beauty of the souls of its people.

CHAPTER 4

A MATTER OF PERSPECTIVE

My biological father often tried to come to my grandparents' house to look for me. However, he was always drunk. I remember everyone wanted to kick him out, thinking they were protecting me. They didn't want me to be left with a lifelong image of an alcoholic father, but he was persistent. I remember one specific time he showed up drunk, and my grandmother wouldn't allow him to see me. He yelled at her, "Open the door, I brought something for my daughter."

She wanted to believe in him. However, when she opened the door, she saw he brought bottles of vodka. For him, that was his idea of a gift—it was all he had to offer. In his drunken state, he didn't realize it was completely absurd to give a child a bottle of vodka. So, of course, my grandmother didn't allow him near me.

She told him, "If you want to see your daughter, come sober and then you can see her as much as you want, but I will not allow you to see her if you are drunk."

Another time, he seemed okay, so my grandmother let him in. She asked me to come out from under the bed, where I was hiding. I did that each time I heard that he was coming. We had those old-fashioned beds with higher legs, so there was plenty of space for me to get under it. I felt safe and secure under there, where I imagined that nothing could hurt me. When I didn't respond, she called my name and asked me again to come out.

I said, "No, I don't want to see him."

After lengthy negotiations, I finally came out. I actually remember that very well. By then, I was around seven years old. I approached him cautiously and he told me, "Come see your daddy, I have something for you."

I went to him. He took me in his arms, kissed me, and told me how much he missed me. Then he handed me money and said for me to buy myself something just for me—candy or toys. He gave me the money in front of my grandparents and extended family, so everyone was happy to think that maybe he finally understood and was changing for the better. My grandmother thanked him for his kindness to me and even asked him to have dinner with us. That was the only day in my entire life that I spent quality time with him—at least that's what I thought at the time.

At the end of the day, when I went out to the car with him to see him off, he hugged and kissed me. Then he asked me where the money was that he had given me earlier. He asked me to show it to him, so I took the money out of my pocket and held it out proudly in my hand.

He said, "Listen, give me back this money and tell me what you want Daddy to bring for you the next time and I will buy it for you."

I believed him and gave him the money back.

I said goodbye with a smile, excited that my daddy would be coming back with a lot of treats for me. I felt so lucky!

Later, my grandmother asked me, "Arnia, darling, where did you put the money that your father gave you?"

I said, "Grandma, he took it back to bring more gifts for me next time."

My grandmother was visibly upset but didn't say anything to me—she was always trying to protect me. By her actions for years to come, it was clear that she had made her decision not to allow me to be subjected to those circumstances. I never saw any gifts from him, and he didn't come back for a long time. And when he finally did, he was drunk. I hid in my safe place under the bed once again. My grandmother never allowed him in the house again.

It is so easy for a child to be manipulated. It is so easy to believe another person's words, especially when it is someone we are supposed to be able to trust. Once we are adults, we can see that those experiences had an impact on us, but by then, we have the capacity to understand that it does not mean that is who that person really is. Trust is one of the most important things that we can have in our life. And, as they say, actions always speak louder than words.

For many years, I couldn't forgive my father for what he did to my mother and to me. I didn't even want to hear his name mentioned. When people asked me about him, I always said that he was dead, and I would give my stepfather's name (even though my father was still living at that time). I rejected him for more than twenty years, until I realized that rejection doesn't allow me to accept reality, which only brings me more sadness and a sense of not belonging. There were times in my life when I felt that I was losing the *joie de vivre* (joy of living) that I used to have—times where I couldn't find my excitement and zest for life.

As I became an adult, I started to question what my life would have been like if I had grown up with my father. The truth is that I don't want to imagine what my psychological health would be like now. I am infinitely grateful to my mother for her decision to leave the situation and make positive changes in our lives, no matter the challenges it presented.

Perspective

Years ago, I began talking to a therapist about these issues. She asked me to tell her about my father. I told her I didn't have a lot to say. And what she said next stuck with me to this day. She explained that if I wanted to improve my own personal life and live in peace, then it was better for me to accept and understand it—all of it. That was it! That was why I couldn't ever seem to move on. I was trying to shut it out, but you simply can't do that. It was from that day forward that my feelings began to change about my relationship with my father, stemming from a deep desire to change my own life. It began to change my perspective.

I decided to talk about him with my family and I began to understand things from his perspective. I became interested in why people drink instead of just looking at what happens after they drink in excess, as I always had. I asked questions that made me look for the reasons that he was in so much pain that he tried to drown himself in alcohol. I still don't have all the answers, but I changed my perception of how I saw things, and slowly, day by day, with a strong will to change my life, I changed my perception of him. In doing so, I ultimately changed the direction of my life.

I also began to accept that he was my biological father, and if he could have done better, I had to believe that he would have. Unfortunately, he didn't know how to do better. How can we expect more of someone, if they don't know how to give what is needed or they don't know how to go about doing any better? You simply cannot give what you don't have.

With this understanding, I try to believe there are no bad fathers or bad parents. Everyone is trying to do the best they can, with the level of awareness they have. Now I understand that my father did what he could do. I can't say that he didn't think of me, because he did—all of his life, he kept coming to visit me. But again, alcohol was all that he had to offer. I believe that he loved me, but he saw things differently. When I understood that he was rejected everywhere he went—when I understood that he wasn't loved, then I began to understand that he needed love more than anyone else.

It's not easy to see things differently. It's not easy to open your vision enough to see different perspectives that people may have. But when you do, you begin to understand your own vulnerabilities and perception of situations more clearly. That's when you start to see light at the end of the tunnel.

CHAPTER 5

THE IMPORTANCE OF ROLE MODELS

Growing up in our small village, without a father and far away from my mother, my grandmother and grandfather became my role models. And without a doubt, thanks to them, I am the woman I am today. I am beyond grateful for them. They instilled in me their own values of life—being respectful, thinking of others, and loyalty. But the most important thing they taught me was to have courage and never, ever give up. In retrospect, they were trying to prepare me to avoid living the life of abuse my mom was living. They were trying to prepare me to be a strong, independent woman who could stand on her own two feet, and they did.

When I was a child and I would be upset about something, they didn't coddle me, saying, "Oh, my poor girl ... what's wrong?" Instead, they would tell me it's nothing and to get up and continue to play or get on with whatever I was doing. When I'd say something was hurting, they would tell me, "It's okay, you will forget it before long." While it may seem a bit harsh to some, I am grateful for their reactions. That attitude molded me into a strong and courageous woman.

At times, my grandmother was also my fun playmate. When I was a small child and was sad or lonely because I didn't have many friends in our small village, she would tell me, "I will play with you." We played all sorts of things, but I especially remember playing with her in the snow and throwing snowballs. It was so much fun! I also remember thinking how amazing it was that with everything she had to do and all her responsibilities, she always made time for me. I was always her priority.

She was also my cooking teacher (even though my grandfather taught me how to eat a traditional Armenian soup called *khash*). Back then, a girl's education was different from a boy's—a girl had to know how to cook, do laundry, and maintain a clean and comfortable home. My grandmother believed that if I got married, I needed to excel at all these skills to take care of my husband and family (and added that it would keep my mother-in-law happy). But my grandmother knew all too well that even if I didn't get married, I would be able to properly care for myself with these skills. I have always loved food, so I was happy to have the opportunity to learn to cook. And some of my very favorite memories include us in the kitchen together, aprons on, laughing and tasting her delicious food.

My grandparents also taught me the value of hard work. Every year, we needed to work especially hard from March to October in the gardens. We would also go into the backwoods to harvest the wild blueberries, raspberries, and blackberries to make delicious jams and jellies. This was done to ensure we'd have enough food for the long, cold winter when the lands and everything on them were frozen solid.

We didn't have the money to go on vacations or anything extravagant like that. My grandparents only had a small pension, enough to buy flour (to make bread), sugar, coffee, oil, and the things that we couldn't grow in the garden. Otherwise, we planted potatoes, green beans, tomatoes, and peppers. We even had three fruit trees that bore apples, plums, and walnuts. We were rich in so many ways that most people simply take for granted.

Before winter was upon us, I would go with my grandpa into the forest to cut enough wood to keep the house warm and to use for cooking. Grandfather was an early riser—he always believed in starting his day at the crack of dawn (or sooner). "Those who sleep late lose the best part of the day," he would say, and then added, "You can sleep when you are dead." Those cold mornings provided many warm, wonderful, cozy moments that I will never forget. I remember helping my grandfather when he cut the trees, bringing them home and helping him prepare the wood for the winter. When I told him I was tired, his answer was, "No, you are not tired. It is only in your mind. Continue, and soon we will have a break."

When I'd say again that I didn't want to continue to work because I was tired, again he told me, "You don't give up—you started something, you finish it. It doesn't matter how tired you are."

And he added, "If each time in your life you start something, and then give up because you are tired, you will never arrive at your destination—you will never achieve anything in your life."

As a child, I didn't understand the meaning of those words. I was getting angry and frustrated because he didn't seem to care when I told him that I was tired. At home, I even complained to my grandma. Now, I look back on those words and realize what a treasure they were. He was teaching me to be courageous and perseverant. Now, I understand that he was giving me the skills and attitude to be able to overcome the challenges of life. At the time, I didn't know what he was doing, but today, I am so grateful he didn't give in to me.

I also started to work at a very young age, not for money for myself, but to help make the burden easier on my grandparents. I was always with them and the other adults. They were all my friends, but my best friends were my grandfather and grandmother. They never betrayed me. They are with me still even today in spirit. They taught me how to work hard and be proud of that work. They showed me that nothing in life comes for free, but if we really want something, we can work toward it. They showed me what it means to have goals and a good, strong work ethic.

But role models can be found all around us, not only in our own homes. I still remember our neighbor who lived just up the hill. I used to call her Auntie, but she was so much more to me—a wonderful person with an even more wonderful, giving, lovely heart. Every day after school, I would go to her place. It was like a second home for me. Her niece and nephew were living there as well, so we played together often. And she, too, taught us how to cook ethnic foods and how to work the land. I loved how caring she was; it didn't matter if you were related or not.

This was also true of a dear friend—and I didn't have many of them growing up. I don't know why really. When I started school, I tried to make friends, but I wasn't very successful at it. I was rejected over and over again. And I knew I didn't need a lot of friends, but I kept thinking one or two would have been nice. I just wanted to find "my person"—someone I could trust and rely on, but also someone with whom I could have fun.

And then I met her. Her name was Ela, and she was in my class. We developed a friendship that would last for years.

Neither of us had a lot, but what we did have, we shared openly and happily. We shared our joy, laughter, sadness, hunger, tears, anger, and even some arguments. But through it all, we had an unconditional love for each other that was stronger than anything that could tear us apart. We were able to keep our friendship despite the distance and all the challenges we faced later in life because we accepted each other as we were without judgment. We were honest and gave pure love without expecting anything in return. This is the secret to our over thirty years of friendship that I prefer to call 'family-ship.' We did a lot of crazy things together, childish things at times, but no one was ever hurt by any of them. I came to understand that everything—food or experiences—shared with honesty, integrity, and a pure love taste wonderfully delicious.

These neighbors and friends became family. And without even knowing it, gave me a beautiful gift. That is, when faced with a difficult situation, I knew I could stand up to it with force and take action because I knew they were behind me. I took that experience and used it as my strength to move forward in my life. I will always remember those who welcomed me with open arms and gave me love, took care of me, protected me, and nourished me. They were always there for me, as if I was part of their family. I looked up to each one of them.

Role Models

A role model is "a person whose behavior in a particular role is imitated by others." When someone, and in particular, a child, has a positive role model to look up to, they are more likely to act similarly to that person. This is a major key to development, as it helps to form new perspectives, habits, and thought processes. Role models set examples of how to behave. These examples may have to do with living a certain lifestyle, increasing self-awareness, demonstrating respect, and showing an unwavering commitment to values and goals.

My grandparents were my role models. They were my teachers, my playmates, my second parents—my everything. Simply, they were my world. And they were very different. For as open and loving as my grandmother was, my grandfather was closed and showed no emotion. Most of the older generation at that time didn't have the words to express their love verbally. It was just not something that was commonly done. Like my grandfather, to them, it was obvious—they didn't have to talk about love. Working so hard to provide for our needs was, indeed, an act of love. And I knew, without a doubt, how much he loved me—no words needed.

I consider myself a lucky woman to have had two mothers in my life, who each gave me unconditional love and prayers. I still believe even today that my grandmother is with me in spirit. And I was blessed to have been given evidence. One day, I was lying on my bed because I wasn't feeling well. I remember crying in the silence, and I felt that I was half asleep and half awake. I saw my grandmother sitting next to me. She caressed my head and said, "Don't cry, Arnia. I am here, I am with you. I will always be with you, so you needn't cry. All will be good." I opened my eyes and felt so much better. I felt her presence and was so relieved knowing I wasn't alone at all. That simple belief allowed me to feel good and move on. In my experience, I have come to realize that what we believe, we create, because every creation is coming from that belief. In this case, I created the peace and joy in my heart from my belief that my grandmother was there for me.

I am grateful that my grandparents taught me what they believed to be the most valuable lessons in life and the importance of being independent. They always told me, "If you want something, work for it. Never wait for someone to give it to you. If they give you something today, tomorrow they may expect something that you are not prepared to give, or they may throw it back in your face. If there is something you want, work for it with honesty and integrity so that when you put your head on the pillow at night, you will have nothing to reproach yourself about and no regrets."

I am also grateful to my role model Ela for showing me the true meaning of friendship. As I have made friends over my lifetime, I always strived to be the friend that Ela was, and still is, to me—the friend I needed at the time and the friend who I supported and loved equally for years.

CHAPTER 6

A SISTER'S LOVE

My childhood wasn't all bad. There were, of course, my loving grandparents and my mom (when I could spend time with her), but having a sister is a gift and one of the richest blessings I have been fortunate enough to have in my entire life. We didn't really grow up together, but it didn't stop us from loving each other and being there for one another throughout our lives. It didn't necessarily start out that way, though. We always loved each other, of course, but we didn't really have a close relationship. I was living in the village with my grandparents when she was born and since I only went to Mom's house in the city once in a while during school vacations, I missed out on growing up with her.

We got to know each other once I moved back to Mom's when I was sixteen years old. And like siblings do, we occasionally fought (which Mom hated). In the beginning, we fought over whose turn it was to do the chores, and as we grew up, it was over her borrowing my clothes without asking. (There were a lot of things we shared, but I preferred that my clothes were not one of them!) Mom used to tell us that she didn't want to hear the word 'mine' because we were sisters and she expected us to share everything. She always wanted us to have a close and loving relationship. Mom insisted that, as the oldest, I was the one who had to set an example for her. And I took that responsibility very seriously.

We always thought of each other as full sisters, even though we had different fathers. Even today, she doesn't call me by my name—instead, she calls me "sister" in Armenian—*Kurik*. I am her *Kurik*, even if she is upset with me, and she is mine. In fact, when she calls me by my actual name, I know she is really angry with me, which is rare.

Like me, my *Kurik* didn't have the best childhood. Her father (my stepfather) didn't treat her well. She was just five years old when he passed away, so she was only exposed to his violence for a short time, thankfully. But, truly, for a child, a minute with an abuser can feel like a year. And sadly, that is what it felt like for her.

Mom tried to play the roles of both father and mother to us. My sister and I didn't have the privilege of doing things together, like going to dance classes or going on vacation together. I was preoccupied with work and helping Mom with responsibilities. I had to help contribute to the household so that we could have the bare minimum of necessities. Many years ago, as a young girl, my sister told me that I was like a second mother to her.

Today, I can say that all three of us went on "as usual," but each had been suffering in silence because we wanted to protect each other. And at the same time, we didn't know how to help one another. Being without a father had been kind of normal for me growing up, so back then, I didn't know how to help her get through that transition. But I reminded her that she had Mom.

My sister shared with me later that she always shared her feelings with Mom, and they would cry together. As a big sister, I only knew that I had to work to help Mom. In our home, we didn't say "I love you"—that phrase was kind of taboo (likely passed down from my grandfather). I knew that we loved each other and were always there for each other, but we never, ever said it. Words didn't seem to be needed, as it was clearly evident that we loved each other. Although, it is nice to hear it once in a while. Being adults, everything changed. We each worked more on ourselves, and we got to know each other authentically and build a true sister relationship. Now, we tell each other that we love each other every time we talk.

My sister is my life. She is my everything, and I can't imagine life without her. Even though she is seven years younger than me, I know that I can ask her opinion and get her perspective on any topic. I call her for everything—when I am happy, when I am sad, when I need advice. She is not only my sister, but my best friend, my advisor, my psychologist, my world. She is not good at answering her phone—often her response to my call or messages may come three days later. If I text her, "How are you?" she may eventually respond days later with, "I am good, how are you?" But I have come to realize that if she doesn't answer me right away, it usually means all is well. My *Kurik* is very intelligent, with an open heart. She blessed me with two beautiful nieces and one nephew and honored me as Godmother for all three of them.

Love and Strength in a Common Bond

I understand that these special relationships are rare. It isn't always like that with everyone, of course, because sometimes people (classmates, neighbors, co-workers, family members, or others) are stuck in the mode of judgment and expectation. As I mentioned, I wasn't always welcomed by other people—quite the contrary. I was mostly rejected and unwanted as a child. I can remember when some people used to say that I was an orphan, that I was a child of an alcoholic father. Later, as an adult, I questioned who could love or respect an alcoholic. So then, how could they love me? Sometimes it's easier for people to judge than to give love. I don't know the reason, but today, I can say that it didn't kill me, nor did it weaken me. Rather, this judgment made me stronger.

My sister and I have more than our mother's blood in common and more than a partially shared upbringing and Armenian heritage. We share the bond of abuse survivors. I don't like to call us victims because I would rather focus on the positive attribute of surviving, just like we did. Just like Mom did. That is a bond that runs deep and will always be there for us.

We must find strength and courage and determination in ourselves, but we also can find them in the support and love of those with whom we have a bond. I found that in my sister. But make no mistake, it doesn't have to be a bond of sisters. It doesn't even have to be familial. When you have someone who loves you unconditionally and without question, someone upon whom you can rely unequivocally, allow them to help you on your journey, just as you would offer to help them.

With time, I began to understand that no one can make us feel "less than" if we don't allow them to. No one can tell us if we are worthy of love. We know we are because we love ourselves. And that's the key. We must learn to love ourselves—the good, the bad, and the ugly—our strengths and our weaknesses—before we can truly love anyone else. We must understand that we have all that we need inside us. And yes, while we all long to be accepted and loved by others, we should remember that all the love we need is truly inside us. We were born with this love. It doesn't matter what we experience in life when we remember that the source of love is always right within us.

I stopped paying attention to the jokes and ridiculing, to the rejection and snide remarks. I let it be as it was. I didn't even try to change things. I just ignored it and didn't give any meaning to it. Subconsciously, I accepted the situation as it was and spent my time being with those who wanted to be with me. That does not mean that it didn't hurt—of course, it did. And often, it hurts even more when you are an adult. As a child, you are more resilient naturally and can bounce back from these setbacks, as I did after being abused so badly. However, as an adult, we question other people and their intentions more.

We also begin to work on ourselves and can make the decision to 'delete' or replace those feelings of rejection. We come to understand that now everything is different, and that we are as worthy as other people—that we are as valuable and as lovable as anyone else. When we change our way of thinking about ourselves and our past situations, we can begin to love ourselves even more. And then our life changes. It takes continuous work, but it is worth it.

The power of love in life is one of the greatest powers of all. We are love, our essence is love, and we are made of love. And it all starts by loving ourselves. When we love ourselves, we can feel it, we can live it, and we can also know what it is. We are not talking about an egotistical conceit type of love. The ego is constantly saying, "Me, Me, Me! I am better than you!" Ego is arrogance. And that is not what this is. Here, we are talking about the pure, unconditional love that starts on the inside and goes out. Self-love is sharing without expectation, giving without manipulation, thinking that we are all one, and treating others the way we want to be treated. We can give love unconditionally and generously. But we cannot love ourselves if we don't first know who we are. It is about accepting ourselves completely. It doesn't matter where we are in our lives, where we are coming from, what we did, what our current situation is, or how old we are; we can make a decision right now to make the change we want in love.

As Neale Donald Walsch says, "What would love do now?" This is key because only with love can we accept, understand, and forgive others. This is, by far, the biggest lesson I have learned in my life. Love is the answer for every situation.

CHAPTER 7

FINDING LIGHT
IN THE DARKNESS

There's no doubt that violence filled much of my childhood. But not everyone believes in violence, even if their family members do. My step-aunt, step-uncle, and step-grandfather were always kind to me, even as their brother and son, respectively, beat us. Isn't it amazing how, in the same family, people can be so very different? That's because it always comes down to what's inside a person, not who they call brother, son, father, or mother. Is there love and understanding or jealousy and judgment? Is there joy and peace or turmoil and doubt?

My step-grandfather showed no favoritism toward the other children in the house and treated me like I belonged in his family. When I was a teenager, I went to live with my mom, sister, and him. My stepfather and step-grandmother had already passed away by then, and my step-uncle, step-aunt, and cousins had moved to another country. So, there were four of us in the house, and he was always very kind and generous. I remember him coming home after work with chocolate or chewing gum for my sister and me. He never treated me any differently than my sister, who was his biological grandchild. Instead, he went above and beyond to make me feel loved and wanted. This was the exact opposite of what I experienced from his wife and son. It was almost as if he was trying to make up for all the pain his son had inflicted on me and Mom over the years.

One of my favorite memories of him happened one day after he came home and hung up his jacket in the foyer, as usual. A bit later, he asked me, "My daughter, would you go get my packet of cigarettes out of my pocket?"

I was always taught that you never go into people's pockets, even if it is a family member and even if they give you permission. With that in mind, I said, "Okay, I'll bring your jacket and you can take it out."

He said, "No, go ahead."

"No, Grandpa, I will bring it to you."

Again, he said, "No, I am telling you to go and bring my cigarettes from my jacket pocket."

I felt badly, but he insisted, so I did it. I went to check the first pocket and found nothing. I came back empty-handed and confused.

Then, he said, "Yes, they are in there, check the other one."

I did, and still nothing.

He said, "Well, check the inside pocket then."

I did and still didn't find cigarettes, but I did find something else: nail polish. He had brought me a gift and was trying to surprise me. I had seen the same dark brown nail polish about a week before in the store and asked Mom if I could have it. She had said no because we couldn't afford silly things like nail polish. It was true that we needed to save every bit of money to buy food, so as disappointed as I was, I understood her response.

My step-grandpa was still working, but his pay was very little. When he did get paid, nearly all of it went to buying groceries. At that time, Mom was selling whatever she could to make money. When Grandpa gave me the nail polish, she was so touched and appreciative. It was much more than nail polish to her—it was the act of kindness and love that meant the most. He said, "Of course, my granddaughter can have nail polish! The other girls are *not* better than her!"

"Enjoy it," he told me.

I was so happy! I hugged him and painted my nails immediately.

A Shining Light

To this day, this is one of my favorite memories with my step-grandfather, but not because I got a gift. It is one of my favorite memories because I remember how I felt—loved and considered and safe, feelings I didn't get to experience often. This gesture made me feel like he truly cared about me. It made me think that even in a house that had so much darkness, there can still be light—an important reminder to us all at any stage of life.

No matter how much darkness surrounds us, we must always try to find the light. It is there in any given situation, even when it is as dark as night. I promise you—it is there. Sometimes, we must work hard to find it. Other times, we must wait for long periods to start to see it shine through. But make no mistake, it will show itself. As we navigate our way through the darkest moments of our lives, remembering that light helps us to ease the burden. The key is to have faith and believe that it is there, and it will find you.

Unfortunately, I am not the only one who has experienced darkness. Darkness is especially difficult for children because they have no options—they have no free will. They cannot choose to leave. Where would they go? It's also more difficult because these are the years their entire being is molded and shaped. All they know is unconditional love and trust. And in these situations, those they instinctively love and trust are often the ones hurting them most. So, on top of the bruises, on top of the yelling and screaming, they are confused about what love means and who they can really trust to stop the pain.

I know from Mom that her life in that house with her second husband was difficult, to say the least. There was daily abuse in the form of physical, mental, or emotional violence. Mom didn't get a divorce this time because she was worried that she would be seen as the one with the problem. After all, it had now happened with two different men. Her husband had gotten very sick by that time and her heart would simply not allow her to abandon him when he needed her most. That's my mom. So, she made a conscious choice to accept that this was her life.

Despite all that she went through, I feel that my mother gave me life (and light) twice—once when I was born, and second, when she made the decision to allow me to live with my grandparents. It was not easy for her to be far away from me.

She wasn't able to see me grow up. She wasn't able to participate in my daily life. Instead, she sacrificed all those moments with me just to know that I was safe. That was the most important thing to her, as it is for most mothers. That's a mother's love. In a perfect world, a child's safety would be found with them, but as we all know, this is not a perfect world. I am both proud of and thankful for her.

CHAPTER 8

IN PURSUIT OF A NEW LIFE

Like many people, I dreamt of being successful. Those dreams helped me get through some tough times—and I wasn't alone. My mother sought success as well. And to help find it, she made the decision to move us to France for a better life. Mom had become a widow at forty-two years of age when my stepfather passed, and she was now alone with two young girls. At that time, we didn't realize that we were writing a new chapter in our lives, one that we continue to be grateful for to this day.

In Armenia, we struggled greatly. I remember Mom couldn't even find a job that paid enough to buy groceries. So, she tried selling homemade yogurts, fresh fish from the fish market, clothing, and shoes. With no car, she had to carry heavy bags door to door to try to sell enough for us to have a meal the next day. She would walk around for up to eight hours trying to sell anything she had to anyone, no matter the weather. I went with her to help as much as I could. This was just one reason we said *goodbye* to the land of our birth and *hello* to a new life in France.

Mom just couldn't see a future for us in Armenia and was ready to get as far away from her past as possible.

I remember the day we finally boarded the plane for Paris—the first day of February 2001—with 100 Franc in our pocket. Our vivid imaginations painted a picture of us landing right next to the Eiffel Tower, with an accordionist playing "La Vie En Rose" by Edith Piaff. With our eyes filled with stars, we landed at Charles de Gaulle Airport. We went outside and looked for the person who was picking us up from the foyer (residential building for immigrants) in which we would be living. We put our suitcases in the car and headed to the small town two hours from Paris that would be our new home.

Within a few short months, we began to discover what our new life looked like through the people, culture, and food we experienced each day. We loved eating our meals in the foyer cafeteria where we were living. And I clearly remember that at one of those meals, we realized how very different cultures could be. In Armenia, it was considered good manners to politely refuse what was first offered. We wanted to be faithful to our education and culture, so, when the waitress came up to us, we simply said, "No, thank you." We assumed she would offer us food again, as was the custom in Armenia, but she never came back! We looked at each other in confusion and then just laughed. Mom told us, "Okay, kids, the next time someone offers you something, you take it and say thank you. Don't wait for them to ask again." In that moment, we had subconsciously started to adapt to our new culture, just as immigrants do every day in all different countries.

It was different than what we were accustomed to, to say the least. We had a table, but it was self-service—everyone got their tray and got in line for the buffet. We didn't recognize many of the foods though and were skeptical. Mom told us to just take a bite to taste and see if we liked it. Soon, we came upon a bowl of green fruit that we had never seen before. We looked at each other, questioning what it was, but no one knew. Mom suggested we each take one to try it. Back at the table, we didn't even know how to eat this mysterious fruit. We discreetly looked around to watch how other people cut and ate it, and then we repeated the gesture. At first, we didn't find it to be very tasty. It seemed to be a rather strange fruit, as it was not sweet at all. Now, it makes sense because it was the first time in our lives that we had sampled avocados!

We met a lot of people at the foyer, especially immigrants just like us from other countries. It seemed that they too felt like they were discovering a new world. Communication with them and everyone else was difficult, as none of us spoke French. Mom remembered some words from her high school French class, but my sister and I couldn't even say our names properly in French. Eventually, I learned to say *bonjour* and I was so happy I knew a word that I started saying it each time I met someone morning, afternoon, and evening. Then, one day, I was informed that it is not appropriate to say it in the evening. Instead, you're supposed to say *bonsoir*. I didn't understand the meaning, so then I started to say *bonsoir* all day. I remember thinking—*Hmmm, this language barrier is going to be harder than I thought.*

Despite the newness of food and language, these were enchanting times in our life. We were immigrants filled with happiness, joy, laughter, and discovery, exploring the language, culture, and delicious food, but there was also some confusion and fear. I remember the first time that we finally discovered the famous Eiffel

Tower—most people's dream. There were tourists all over the place, jostling each other to take photos. There were merchants selling every type of souvenir of the Eiffel Tower imaginable, French cafes with their outdoor terraces, and French artists lining the streets painting picturesque landscapes. We couldn't go to a cafe or a bistro because we didn't have the money. So, we would gaze at the people sitting at those quaint round tables and tell ourselves that one day, we too would be sitting there eating a croissant.

Mom bought us two sandwiches from a vendor under the Eiffel Tower and we divided them in three. They were delicious! We were simply in awe of everything around us. We enjoyed them and were proud that we too were able to eat in Paris, especially beneath the Eiffel Tower. Each bite was a source of pride, joy, accomplishment, and adaptation. We now felt like we were in the big leagues, just like the Parisian films we had heard about. We were in our own movie, living our moment on one of our first paths to our new life.

I remember the first time we visited the district known as Montmartre—a place every tourist wants to visit. We saw the majestic Basilica de Sacré Coeur located at the summit of the city, also known as the original artists' quarter—*Quartier des Artistes*, with its lively narrow streets and French bistros and shops. It was all so incredibly beautiful! It almost had its own heartbeat. During our visit, we heard a captivating melody that sounded like it was coming from far away. We all started looking around and walked in the direction of the sound. Soon, hiding behind the branches of a tree, we discovered a Monsieur sitting with an accordion and playing the music of Edith Piaff's "La Vie En Rose."

We did not believe what we were seeing with our own eyes. We realized our dreams were coming true before our very eyes, right down to the music we imagined playing in this majestic land. I loved my life in France, a country that I cherish and will keep in my heart forever. I adopted it first subconsciously and then consciously as my own country. To this day, I consider myself as much French as Armenian. So, I will agree with my compatriot, Charles Aznavour, when he said, "I am 100% French and 100% Armenian." I can't make a choice because the two countries both make me proud to be a citizen. But I can say that I have enough love in my heart for both.

Transformations

What we didn't realize during this glorious time was that we were transforming, but not just in language and not just in learning about new foods. Our thoughts were changing, our feelings were shifting, our perspectives were widening. These are the amazing transformations that happen when you are exposed to a different way of life and when you allow yourself to open up to the new possibilities it brings with it. This is never truer than when you have been closed off for so long due to your prior circumstances.

This is where true growth happens for us all. We must not be scared of the transformation that is occurring, but instead, welcome it with open arms as the necessary next step to get where we want to go. We will never truly grow and understand more about ourselves if we stay in the same circumstances, afraid of change. In order to truly transform, we must have the ability to see the opportunities that are before us. We must take a risk, which can be scary. And we must see it through. Just like my beloved grandpa used to tell me over and over again, we cannot quit, no matter how tired we are. This is the strength, determination, and beauty of transformation.

CHAPTER 9

GROWTH AND DETERMINATION THROUGH CHALLENGES

Just when you begin to think you're finally making progress, you may get hit with another challenge or setback. In fact, you likely will—we all will. And sometimes that challenge is dressed as rejection. This is especially difficult for abuse victims, who already have long-stemmed feelings of rejection due to the violence they previously endured.

When we arrived in France, I wanted to go to school. But I was too old for junior high, so social services contacted the high school on our behalf. I remember when the social services lady hung up the phone and matter-of-factly told my mom that since I was a newcomer who could not properly speak French, I would have a hard time integrating myself into school. They wouldn't even give me a chance or test me to see at what level I could speak or understand French. We felt deflated but would not give up (it was not in our nature). My mom very much wanted me to get my education. So, we kept calling the school to try to find a solution. I recall the day when that call proved too much for me to take. The woman who picked up the phone told social services, "Stop insisting! This school is not a dump for garbage to be brought into." It felt like another slap in my face—just as painful as all those I suffered as a child.

I stopped pursuing my dream that day. Despite the social worker's best efforts, I could not finish my high school education. Instead, I went to training workshops to take courses to improve my French and to find work. It was in one of those workshops where I met someone who would finally be on my side. My French language teacher encouraged and supported me during this time. She also encouraged me to enroll in the college's floral design program. Madame Colette is an exceptional woman. She was the perfect example of generosity and kindness, giving so much love to those around her without expecting anything in return.

She touched my life, and without a doubt, many more lives—it was simply her nature. After twenty years of friendship, I consider her a part of my family. She always believed in me, even when I didn't believe in myself. And she changed the trajectory of my life in France. Thanks to her, I went on to do the CAP (*Certificate Aptitude Professionelle*) and became a florist. She was determined to help me not only take these steps, but also see that I could do it, and that it was the correct path for me to take. She encouraged me to go to school, even though I kept telling her that I couldn't because I didn't speak French very well and feared I would fail. However, trusting her and her advice was the best decision I ever made, and I am grateful to this day for it.

By the end of 2001, I found work as a florist while attending school for two more years. At that time, my mother was still unable to find work, so we had to live on my 600 Euros per month. For Mom, it was another struggle—an immigrant trying to find work in a new country she barely knew. She recalls that wherever she went, most employers told her that she was too old or simply that there was no work. She occasionally found small jobs such as housecleaning or picking fruit, and would work part-time as they needed her. I saw my mom struggle to find a real job. She wanted permanent employment and a fresh beginning, too. She needed it as much, if not more, than I did. One day, she had had enough. She got very angry with social services, who refused to help her. She took her file with all the documents organized precisely that showed every single place that she had gone to ask for work. She said she finally put everything on the table in front of the social services lady that was assigned to help her. With tears in her eyes, she said, "Now, is this enough? Are you really going to help me find work? I need it! I can't continue like this anymore."

Mom remembers that the lady looked at her and said apologetically, "I'm sorry, Madame, we didn't know that you were serious about your search for work."

The next day, she got an interview and was hired at a factory. She works there to this day. What I remember most about this time is *not* the challenges we faced, but our fierce determination never to give up—and how that determination paid off in the end.

Attitude and Determination – Never Quitting

We look longingly toward our future, creating a heaven in our mind's eye that we expect to be easy or at least easier than what we left. The very idea of not having to continuously struggle is motivation in and of itself. But we forget to envision the reality.

We often fail to imagine what it will truly take to manifest our dreams. In cases such as these, it seems that anything is better than where we are and would be worth the risk. We sometimes don't realize that there is nothing easy about it. First, we must find the ways and means to do so. Then we have to start over from scratch, learning a new language and a new culture. Yet there is something about human nature that compels us to wonder what we are missing and that perhaps there is something better out there than what we currently have. For many, it is a dream that eventually comes true. And the deciding factor is often determination.

In our case, this was about overwhelming feelings of being rejected in our new country—a country in which we were desperate to start our new lives. The plight of an immigrant is often an uphill battle. We face controversy, hostility, and at the very least, are often misunderstood. As such, it can be a constant challenge. I came to understand that when we make the decision to leave our country, we dream of all the possibilities and of making them all come true, not the challenges of starting over. We have to learn a new language, adopt a new culture, and face the unending prejudices that always seem to be there when someone is "different."

Some people may find it hard to understand the struggles of an immigrant if they have never been immigrants themselves. Upon arriving in a new country, all the things that are important to us—customs, traditions, foods—the things that we hold so dear to our hearts don't matter to all the people in the new country, who have their own cherished traditions. And while they seem to have no value to others, they will always have value in our hearts. This is true even for education or professional status. For example, if you were highly educated in your country and became a doctor or professor, you would say goodbye to that title when you say hello to your new country. To attain that status again, you would have to start over.

From my perspective, we emigrate to a new land for a variety of reasons, mostly because we don't see a future in our own country. It's not because we don't love our country, but because economic or political conditions often dictate it. People are escaping poverty, war, even ethnic violence. They see it as worth the risk to seek a better life elsewhere. Some people risk their lives crossing the sea or the mountains, bringing their dreams right along with them, and many risk losing their lives in search of those dreams.

In my experience, one of the biggest difficulties for an immigrant is being accepted by other people in the new country. It is likely that we are not only bringing our suitcase full of clothing, but we are also bringing the culture, language, history, and even our own story. It is not like we can forget all of this in one day and start to live as a new person the following day. I also think that a lot depends on the age of the person. It is often not as difficult for children to adapt to the new culture, as they are more open to change and less likely to judge differences. While adapting to a new life, families still want to preserve their heritage and their cultural traditions. So, do you choose what you know and love or what the outside world says you should do?

In my case, I decided to make my own choices. First, I was self-aware enough to question myself. *What did I want? And how did I want to live?* There were many cultural aspects of my native country of which I did not agree. So, I decided to leave them behind. I then took the aspects that I felt most aligned with from Armenia and took the parts of the French culture I loved most to make a beautiful mix and create a unique life for myself.

I've found that when we take the time to get to know someone who is different than ourselves, we open up a whole new world and are blessed with the diversity of thought and perspective that they can bring to our lives. We can find that behind the differences are many similarities. Perhaps hiding behind that exterior is a talented artist, a teacher, even a doctor who could one day save your life. If only we could stop judging and accept each other as we are, we may find that the differences are beautiful and that we have a trusted friend who accepts, values, and trusts us in return. And best of all, we can evolve together.

With greater awareness and consciousness, and through my interactions with those who are born in the country, I have also come to understand that immigration can be difficult for them as well. They watch us bring our own cultures and traditions to their homeland. There could also be a fear that if they accept us, they could eventually lose their own identities. Once again, we must look with an empathetic approach. If we were them, would we be willing and able to accept it without prejudice? Or would we be skeptical of foreigners suddenly coming to our homeland, with a fear that our own traditions and sense of unity will be lost?

I would assume that our ancestors did everything they could to keep their cultures alive amidst the temptations that new cultures presented. I think there are many in every culture who may prefer not to venture out of their comfort zones, where it is "safe." It may be because they love what they have, that they are fearful of being misunderstood by others or rejected, or simply because they are content as they are. I don't think there is anything wrong with any of those choices, as long as we find harmony, peace, and joy within us.

When we are open to learning how to serve and accept each other's values, we can use our differences and the value of each individual and their gifts and talents to our advantage, instead of trying to change each other to our own way of thinking. The similarities do not make us one. I think what makes us one is being together, hand in hand, and our acceptance and celebration of each other. Simply, we are one when we respect our differences and accept each other—flaws and all.

Sadly, I've observed that even as late as recent years, there is still much progress to be made in being open to other cultures. People are often judged by their physical attributes, the clothes they wear, their mannerisms, what they do, and anything else that "stands out." The individual may be evaluated without any time spent to learn who they really are. I am convinced that judging and labeling them creates immediate barriers, so we continue to believe what we believe. But when we label, we are usually wrong.

I have also observed that many people have formed preconceived notions, and thus opinions, based on what they see on television. For example, they may see that hunger, poverty, and disease exist in a different part of the world and then think that it is coming to their country with the immigrants. However, they are being given a biased picture. There is so much more. I can agree that there are parts of the world that are impoverished, but that is the same everywhere. And it never negates the beauty that is also there. They have culture, tradition, and their love and respect for family, the arts, sculpture, dance, and music.

I understand that we are all responsible for the legacy that we will leave to our world. The essential question we may want to ask of ourselves is: What kind of world are we going to leave for future generations? Parents must give their children more than food, shelter, and clothing. They must also give them a vision of what a world looks like without prejudice, hatred, racism, discrimination, and violence.

Even through these often-difficult circumstances, conversations, and awakenings, it comes down to our attitude and level of determination. There is always a solution. You may have to work for it. In fact, you'll likely have to work for it. But it can be done. Sometimes it may not be the right time and we have to wait a while longer or we must consider changing our way of doing things. Determination is actually one of the most important things in life. It drives you until you succeed. It doesn't matter how many obstacles you must face on your way—just like my mom on her quest to find a job.

With the right attitude and determination, one day, you will finally be able to tell yourself, "I did it!" Determination forces you to overcome your own doubts and gives you confidence that you can do it. Asking questions of yourself can help: *Who is it that I want to become because of this situation? Do I want to be a victim or a winner?* Once you answer these questions honestly, you will need to make a choice and from there, take responsibility to change things to create what you want.

We should never give up because the road ahead is difficult. Most of the time, we find it easy to give up, especially when someone tells us no or says it is not possible. Whether you are an immigrant or not, there will always be someone who will not believe in you, who will tell you, "No, you can't, it's not possible." But remember that while there will always be rejection, there will also always be someone who will step up to support your goals and stay in your corner. So, I would say, if you don't believe in yourself, trust the one who believes in you.

CHAPTER 10

FINDING SUCCESS

My mom, sister, and I had never taken a real family vacation. But by 2005, we had finally saved enough money and were going on vacation in the south of France for an entire week! We rented a beautiful apartment on the Mediterranean Sea. It was August, and it was very hot. From Lyon, where we lived, to Menton, where our amazing trip would be, was a five-hour trip by car. I drove my new (to me) car, and the sun was scorching. I opened the window to take in the fresh air. (My "new" car didn't have air conditioning.)

It was noisy with the windows open, so we had to talk louder to each other. But we didn't care. We were on our way to see the beautiful blues of the 'Med' on our first real family vacation—that was all that mattered. But we laughed at how loud we had to yell to each other during that car ride. When we arrived, we saw that our seaside destination was everything we thought it would be … and more. We could even hear the sound of the waves breaking on the breathtaking beach below. I thought I'd found heaven!

The best we could afford was a studio apartment, quite small, but with a balcony and a beautiful view of the sea. There was no air conditioning, but we were on the fifth floor, so we at least had a calming and nearly constant sea breeze. It also had a tiny kitchen, two beds, and a sleeper-sofa. There wasn't much privacy, but we didn't care—we were on vacation! We felt so incredibly blessed to be able to have the experience of a family vacation together for the first time in our lives.

Each day, we woke up and went for a morning swim. We would then have lunch in the city, and every evening, we went to an Italian bistro for creamy, delicious gelato. There were more great moments than I can possibly count—seeing the sights, laughing together, enjoying the calming waves, and watching beautiful sunrises and sunsets, as the sky woke up and then turned in for the night.

Menton was fifteen minutes by car from Monte Carlo, Monaco, and we wanted to see it all! We arrived in our old car (with no air conditioning) right in the middle of luxury overload. All the luxurious cars were lined up outside of big, imposing hotels and the most expensive restaurants. And we pulled up and parked right next to them all. We laughed so hard, even while thinking we were likely the poorest people in Monaco at the moment. We must have been quite a spectacle to others. You could tell with their stares that they were wondering if we got incredibly lost or were just from another planet. But to us, we had finally arrived!

We did a walking tour of the area and visited the Royal Palace, the villas of the stars, and the beautiful boutiques. We went into a coffee shop in front of the big famous casino but didn't realize that two coffees and two sodas would cost us 20 Euros. That was a lot of money for us, so we decided to cancel our plans of eating at a restaurant in Monaco that day.

At the time, I remember thinking that if you have all those luxuries—the cars and homes, and can shop in expensive boutiques, it must mean that you are successful. I thought surely if someone has reached that level of monetary worth, they must have succeeded and met all their goals. You see, I was brought up without much in terms of material items, so I always thought that those meant success. Actually, many people think the same thing, regardless of how they grow up. People have always tended to place too much value on material items and not enough on what truly is most valuable—the things you can't see or touch or snap photos of. Still, at that time, I thought I was not successful. And I wasn't alone.

My mom and sister were feeling the exact same way. We were all wondering if one day, we too could have those beautiful homes or that expensive car or shop in those high-end stores and eat in those delicious bistros. We came back to our apartment with our heads filled with lofty dreams made up of expensive clothes, jewelry, and cars. But what I specifically remember most about that night was that my mom made us a delicious dinner with love, and I remember thinking it was better than any expensive restaurant in the world. I remember thinking that we may not have all those material items, but we certainly had an abundance of inner peace and love in our hearts that we shared together. Isn't that success in and of itself?

What Is Success?

What determines success? What determines success when you have lived in abusive situations? Does moving to another country mean we are successful? Would expensive houses, cars, and clothes mean success? Would taking a vacation mean we had achieved success? These are questions we may ask ourselves.

Over the years, and through many of these types of experiences, I began to understand that the meaning of success truly has nothing to do with what society would have us believe. It is something else entirely. Being successful is when you can see that your life is better now than it was months or years ago, or even the day before. It is about all the things that are inside of you, not those that are external, as so many people think.

For example, if you didn't have work for many years, and now you do, but it is at a dead-end job, you could (and should) consider it a success. Why? Because it allows you to eat and provide for your needs and those of your loved ones. If you have a car (even an old, beat up one with no air conditioning), it is a success because it allows you to get to that job without walking for miles.

In our case, we became successful because we went from having nothing to having everything that truly matters—joy, peace, love, laughter, and safety. Going from the trauma of abuse to a peace of mind that can only be found when you feel safe, secure, and loved is a success that is indescribable. Our life on that vacation was far better than it was before.

It really comes down to gratitude and looking at the positivity in our lives, rather than wallowing in all the negativity. It is our choice. When you can find something that is better today than it was yesterday, you are successful. Period. It has nothing to do with a big, expensive house, car, or yacht. So, yes, being on that vacation was a success because we never could have done it before. In the same respect, likely being the poorest people in Monaco was not a failure. In fact, it was also a success—*we were in Monaco!*

It's also important to recognize that even while we acknowledge each and every success in our lives—no matter how large or small—it's okay to want more success. It's okay to see what else you can manifest in your life. Each of us will have a different take on what comes next. Some will be good with the success they have currently. Others will want more. There is no right or wrong, nor is there a limit. We are the only ones who can determine what success truly means to us. We can even set our goals as high as the sky, as long as we have gratitude for what we have right now.

The key is to understand that happiness is not in the material things. Those things will never truly fulfill the heart. They may be nice, and they may be a lot of fun, but they will never provide love and health. I am not saying there is anything wrong with them. After all, why not, if you can afford them and they increase your happiness, and as long as the absence of them does not make you unhappy because you've become dependent on them. That's the key that people tend to miss.

We must first find the happiness, peace, and success within us. Only then should we seek the material things to add to it. Otherwise, we are doing it backwards. Make no mistake, those things do not define success or happiness. Simply, without the fulfillment of the heart, we are the poorest people on earth … even with millions of dollars. And the really good news? We can have both. One of my favorite quotes by Vivian Greene seems appropriate here …

"Life isn't about waiting for the storm to pass. It's about learning to dance in the rain."

CHAPTER 11

HISTORY WILL TRY TO REPEAT ITSELF, BUT IT DOESN'T HAVE TO

By the time I was an adult, I began to realize that consciously or subconsciously, I was on track to take the same path that my mother had taken. At that time, it wasn't necessarily my priority to get married, have children, or settle into the routine of family life. But I remember saying that if I did marry, I would marry someone of my choosing and with whom I would be able to share everything freely. But of course, most of all, it would be someone whom I would love unconditionally for the rest of my life, and who would love me in the same way.

When I was in my mid-twenties, people began telling me that it was time I got married and had a family. I felt pressure, so when the man who would become my fiancé appeared, I was reassured when I heard that he was a good person from a good family. And I can confirm that he was a good son, brother, and friend. However, that did not mean he would be a good fiancé or a good husband for me, as I would soon discover. When we began seeing each other, he appeared to be kind, friendly, funny, and understanding. But that would soon change.

At some point, I felt like his attitude toward me began to shift. I began to experience a change in his energy that told me he might have been playing a role before. It seems to me that when you are in love with someone and trying to build a relationship to create a future with that person, you don't intentionally sabotage it at its roots. It's like building a house and purposely manipulating the construction of it so that it doesn't have a sound foundation. You wouldn't do that. In any new construction, you ensure that the base is strong enough so that it will weather any storm that approaches.

I believe it to be the same with a relationship. If, in the beginning, you are not honest and are hiding behind a mask or manipulating, there is no hope that the relationship will be a happy one. I feel that was the case for us. After our engagement, things were different. I no longer recognized him. It was obvious to me that he wasn't the understanding, friendly, funny man I thought I once knew.

He began to tell me what I should or should not wear and how I should do my makeup. That was annoying to say the least, but what I could not accept was when those comments turned into violence. I remember the first time he raised his hand to me when we were preparing to go to our friend's house for dinner. We were discussing what to bring and that discussion ended in an argument. And the next thing I knew, he took me by the neck and slammed me up against the wall. I was choking and in shock. I couldn't imagine that he was capable of such violence. I didn't say anything, as I couldn't even speak. Time felt like it was frozen. I was silent and in disbelief—I couldn't even cry.

To keep the peace, we ended up going. We took the bottle of wine and went to our friend's home with big smiles on our faces like nothing had happened. I put on the persona of being in a happy relationship, and no one was the wiser.

After that incident, I continued to be blinded and unable to see all the red flags. I somehow thought it was okay—that it was my fault that I made him angry (which sounded so familiar to me). Since I grew up in that kind of environment, I thought it was my duty to accept it. However, today, I can say that once we close our eyes to it, subconsciously we are sending a message that we are to blame and that their behavior is acceptable. They then feel that they are justified in their actions, so they are likely to do it again. That is exactly what happened, because there were two more instances that occurred—once for my makeup and once for what I was wearing.

I actually tried talking to him about it. I don't know what I thought would happen, but I was still trying. He just claimed it happened because I wasn't listening to him—like that was some sort of excuse! I started thinking to myself, I upset him, so that made it okay to hit me? He told me he was the man of the house, so it would be his right to keep his family in line. As per my subconscious childhood conditioning, I tried to understand the first two times it happened. I remember he would apologize and call me sweetheart, saying, "You made me angry. Listen to me the next time." So, I questioned myself again and thought it was my fault it happened.

I wondered, should I accept everything because that's the way it works, and all couples have this problem? I was lost. Now, not only did I not recognize him, but I no longer recognized myself. I was becoming someone that I didn't choose to be. I was losing my freedom of thought, words, and choices. It was clear—I was to become a submissive fiancée and then a submissive wife.

The third time opened my eyes, though, and I understood that not only was this not normal, but it was definitely not my fault. Even though I may have done something that displeased him, I knew that it did not give him the right to disrespect me or conduct himself in that manner. I respected myself and my body too much to allow it to continue. It occurred to me that if he could be that violent over something trivial, how would he react if we were discussing something much more serious?

I wasn't consciously aware then, but I later realized that there was something inside me telling me that this was not good or normal. I couldn't put it into words. I knew in my heart that something was wrong. I remembered all that my mom went through and I couldn't imagine my life without having the right to express myself or make my own decisions, or to at least have a chance to discuss it with my partner. Shouldn't we be able to make our decisions together? I needed to be able to express myself freely without fear that he would be angry and violent.

By that time, I remember that his violence had escalated to the point that he would raise his hand to me, push me up against the wall, and even try to rip my dress off because it wasn't the one he wanted me to wear. That was the red flag that opened my eyes. *Did I dare to listen to that small voice telling me that something was seriously wrong?* I still wasn't completely sure. And against the odds, we had decided to get married and had already set a date and begun to prepare for the wedding. We even had the documents prepared at city hall.

In my heart, I knew it wasn't the right thing to do, but I didn't dare listen to that voice out of fear. The closer the date got, the unhappier I became. I finally connected to that force and courage that was inside me—that voice that had always been with me every moment of my life—the voice that was telling me that something was wrong. One month before the wedding date arrived, I told him I had made my decision and I was leaving him. Of course, that wasn't easy because I remember that he became verbally abusive and started hitting and throwing furniture around the room. That confirmed my decision. I think that was the best day of my life. That day, I took charge of my life and changed its direction so that I would not follow the same path that Mom had.

Breaking Habits; Changing Patterns

We can call that voice intuition, God, or the Universe—whatever resonates with us. But it is there to help guide us on our path. Silence the chatter and listen to it. You know what you need to do. Deep down, we always know.

With my decision to leave him, I cut the familial path that I was subconsciously taking—becoming an abuse victim because I was the daughter of one. From that day on, I learned to stand up for myself. I had respect for myself. I wished him all the best, and I still do. I hope he finds love and happiness. I understood that no one can give you bread to eat if they don't have it for themselves. No one can give you a glass of water to drink if they are thirsty themselves. For that reason, I am not angry and have no hatred for him. I still have love for him. Not the love between a man and a woman, but just love as a habitant of the earth and a child of the universe. Again, always remember that love is the answer.

I think when two hearts are truly open, the only thing that can be offered is love—pure and unconditional, beautiful love. So, in that state, two people can share even deeper feelings. This is when our hearts can open fully and simply share what's in them without conditions attached.

From this experience, I understood that I am the master of my life with the right to make my own choices. Despite what some people said, and they said a lot, I made the choice to cancel the wedding and leave him. I also made the choice not to live with other people's opinions, and not to live in fear of what the community, society, friends, and neighbors would think of me. That's because I know who I am. No one can give me their happiness, and no one can come wipe away my tears.

From that day on, I decided to be me. Not the me that my family expected, not the me that society insisted upon, not the me that my culture wanted, not the me that my religion demanded, but the me that *I decided to be*. And that is the pathway to happiness. From that day on, I was going to design my future, not allow my past to dictate it.

CHAPTER 12

LOVING AND LETTING GO

In addition to having the most supportive and loving parents, my mother also had the most wonderful siblings. And each of them played a huge role in my life. Like my grandparents and step-grandfather, they were also my light in the darkness.

My uncle, Mom's only brother, was very supportive of us throughout our lives. He leant support to Mom when she was married and always gave her good advice. He tried repeatedly to get both my father and stepfather to understand that the way they were treating us was not right. He encouraged them to be kinder and treat us with respect. He endured many sleepless nights on our behalf and was always there to lend Mom a shoulder on which to cry. He and my aunt (his wife) were there to offer us their support psychologically and physically whenever they could.

I remember one night I was with my mom and my sister. It was the middle of the night, and we awoke to loud noises that we could guess were things breaking and crashing. We saw our mother being beaten again. We remember Mom taking us in our pajamas and pushing us out the front door. She took my sister's hand and told me to run. Since I was older, I could run without help, and we ran as fast as we could so that my stepfather couldn't catch us. We ran all the way to the bus station.

In Armenia, the bus services run twenty-four hours. The bus came—mostly empty in the middle of the night. Mom wiped away her tears, telling the driver that she didn't have her wallet with her and couldn't pay. The driver looked at Mom and said, "Not a problem, Madam. I am not going to ask you for the money." We arrived at my uncle's house in the middle of the night and they welcomed us and gave us all a hug and a bed. We woke up safe and secure in the morning and stayed like that for a few days, but in the end, we couldn't stay there forever. However, when we were there, we felt protected, we felt safe, and we felt loved.

Other times, my uncle would come to visit us at my grandparents' house and bring food and flour for us to make bread. Some of my favorite memories of him were when he would come back from trips to Russia and bring back gifts for my cousins and me. His youngest daughter and I were the same age, and we were very close. My cousins and I grew up together like brothers and sisters. We even fought a lot like siblings—within ten minutes we were playing together again. My uncle was a role model for me. He showed me the type of man I would want to be with one day—one who is kind and caring, with a big heart like his father, my grandfather.

I used to recognize his car from far away. I couldn't wait to run and greet him, jumping up and down with excitement. One day when I was twelve years old, I was experimenting with makeup a friend had given me for the first time. I was alone that day and tried on all the colors of eyeshadow—green, blue, red, and orange. I also had bright red blush and lipstick. When I saw my uncle's car, I put the makeup brushes down and ran to meet him. I'll never forget him opening the car door and seeing my face. He wasn't happy and said, "What is this?" I didn't understand. I had been so proud of myself! I told him that it was my first time wearing makeup, and I did it all by myself. He was unimpressed and told me to go wash it off my face right away and only then would he give me a hug. I asked him if he was sure, because it was nice, and I did it myself. He said, "Yes, I am sure. Now go and clean your face and don't do it again. You are too young! You are not old enough yet to put makeup on your face like that." I went and washed my face and then I finally got my hug.

Each time I saw him, my heart filled with joy. When it was time for him to leave, whether it was just him or he was with my aunt and cousins, I was always devastated. I found myself crying, empty, alone, and sad, and each time, I started to count the days until they would return. When he passed away, it was a great loss to our family.

My mother also had one sister, who I called my 'Italian Aunt Rita' because she lived in Italy. As a child, I would see her when she came to visit us in Armenia. Back then, I didn't know her well, but when we moved to France, I was able to spend more time with her. She was my idol! I wanted to be like her—strong, courageous, funny, smart, intelligent, and brave. I admired the fact that she knew how to stand up for her rights. In my eyes, she was the perfect woman. And we both had the same dream—to become an artist. One day she told me that she went to drama school, but back then it was very hard for a woman to get into theater in Armenia. In the 1970s, any woman who wanted to become an artist was judged, criticized, and unwelcomed. But no one could stifle her intelligence and creativity. When she met her husband, they moved to Italy.

She lived four and a half hours away from us by car once we moved to France. So, I went to Italy as much as I could to spend time with her. Aunt Rita gave me small opportunities when I was there to get a taste of her lifestyle. At that time, I was in my later teens and there was nothing better than spending time with my idol. I spent Christmas, New Year's, Easter, and summers with her. Those were the best years of my teenage life. I learned so much from her. She taught me how to stand up for what I believed in and how to say no if I did not agree with something. And she taught me to never give up on my dreams.

We laughed a lot together! She was even my hairdresser one day, although she had never cut hair in her life. We were kind of bored, so she suggested we cut my hair to give me a new look. A "trim" turned into cutting most of my hair off! We laughed some more when I looked at myself in the mirror. Her husband told us we were both crazy. My hair grew out just fine, but that memory will stick with me forever. Another day, I did her makeup for her, and let's just say, thankfully, there was nowhere she had to go.

I also appreciated her style in fashion. She let me borrow her clothes and taught me how to coordinate my outfits. I remember that I wasn't very good at choosing my own clothes because I had really never done it before. We only got new clothes for school once a year. But she showed me what to do, even with limited pieces.

When doctors diagnosed her with cancer, my mom spent most of her time in Italy to assist with her care. My sister was with me in France. My amazing Aunt Rita passed away at the young age of fifty-one, taking with her the *joie de vivre* (joy of living) and her beautiful smile. She will always be remembered for the legacy she left behind.

On the last day that I saw her in the hospital, I was telling her goodbye because I knew I would never see her again. She knew it as well, but it was unspoken between us. I guess we wanted to protect each other from the reality of that pain, hoping that maybe somehow, it would not happen.

However, she did share her dream for me. She told me, "Arnia, my love," raising her hands to point to the wall of the hospital in explanation, "imagine that point there is your goal and your dream—keep looking at it and keep moving. Whatever happens in life, never give up and if someone tries to stop you, don't allow them. Just keep looking toward your goals and dreams and keep going."

Those were her last words to me. Then she kissed me and told me to go or I would miss my train. I kissed her goodbye, but emotion kept me from saying "I love you." I just didn't say those words back then, although she did—all the time. She knew the power of love and how to express it in her actions and words. So, as a young woman of twenty-two years, I couldn't open my mouth to tell her that I loved her. I know she knew it, but I am telling her now in this way—*I love you, mia Zia Rita!*

Our final goodbye was actually not in the hospital that day. When my sister and I returned to France, I knew that one day soon, Mom would call me with the news that Aunt Rita had left the earth. That night I had a dream in which Aunt Rita was calling to me, "Arnia, come to see me. I want to tell you goodbye. It is time for me to leave."

I said, "I can't right now because I have to buy the train ticket and arrange with my employer to take the weekend off. I will come this weekend."

She said, "No, Arnia, I don't have the time. I am leaving now."

I said, "How can I come now? I don't have a ticket."

Then she answered, "I am leaving now, my Arnia. I just wanted to come to tell you goodbye, I am going now." And her voice in my dream disappeared.

I suddenly woke from my sleep and sat up on my bed. When I looked at the time, it was 4:30 a.m. I was sweating, and I knew that she was gone. A few hours later, Mom called and said that she left us to join her family at 4:30 a.m. I told her that I knew because she had come to tell me her last goodbye.

Letting Go

We lost four family members all with eight months in between them. It started with my grandpa, who, thankfully, had a peaceful death. One morning he woke up early, looked at the forest around him, took a deep breath, and went back to bed, something that was very unusual for him. He passed in his sleep. Eight months later, my uncle had a heart attack, and eight months after that, my lovely Auntie Rita in Italy passed away from cancer. In another eight months, my grandma joined her husband, son, and daughter. There were three siblings, so Mom not only lost her parents, but also her brother and sister. Other than my sister and I, she was alone.

Those four years were the most difficult years for our family. Losing a loved one is one of the hardest things that we will experience in our lifetime. We get through it because we believe they are in a better place. We believe that the soul never dies, and they are with us each time we think about them and each time we remember those great moments that we shared together. We can feel their presence and believe that they are everywhere—they are in the rain, in the stars, in the snowflakes, and in the morning sunshine. We believe that our souls need our bodies to live on this earth, so they just leave the body behind. The soul moves on and lives forever in the ethers.

We have limited control of what life brings us, but we can control our thoughts and actions concerning it. Of course, some days are harder than others. We can't bring them back to this earthly plane, but we can decide to see them in the morning sunshine and in the whisper of the wind. I believe that one day, the time will come when we meet again, all together, and laugh again.

CHAPTER 13

WILLPOWER AND MINDSET

One thing is for sure—if we know what we really want and we are determined, we can make it happen, even if we must cross the ocean to do it. It doesn't matter how long you have wanted it. If you want something badly enough and are willing to work toward your goal, you will likely achieve it.

After many years of working in the client services profession, I decided that I wanted to change careers. I wanted to go to school and learn tourism. Every school was asking me for a high school diploma and the ability to speak the English language well. Of course, I still did not have a high school diploma and at the time, I did not speak English at all. I kept calling all the private and public schools, but the answer was the same from all of them. Only one of them told me that if I could speak English, they could accept me without a high school diploma. They said that because I was an adult, it would be necessary to take an exam to see what level I was at in different subjects, which I found to be fair.

Now that I had a school that was willing to accept me, I knew that I needed to learn English. So, I had the idea that if I went to Canada, it would be easier to learn and then I could come back and go to school. But I had another problem—I did not have the money to do so. I asked everyone if they knew where I could get the money. Someone suggested that I make an appointment with one of the officials of my province to seek advice. When the secretary asked me the reason that I wanted to see the official, I said it was personal, because I feared that if I told her the reason, she would not give me an appointment. I went to my appointment and told the official about my situation and explained why I needed the money. She informed me that there was an association that helped, with minimal participation, anyone who wanted to go to school or start a business. I will never forget that day, as that person changed my life forever. I went to the association and got the funds I needed.

When I arrived in Toronto, Ontario, Canada, I took ESL classes for six months to learn English. I was determined to learn the language as quickly as possible. After that, I started to work in a call center as a bilingual agent. One day, one of my coworkers told me that there was a high school for adults in Toronto, not far from where I was living. I had not known about it, but it turned out to be within fifteen minutes walking distance from my apartment. I was excited to find out more! I enrolled in the school and took a test in English, Mathematics, and Science to see my current levels. I will never forget the day that I was sitting in the admissions office. The lady who interviewed me was asking me specific questions:

"Are you working?"

I said, "Yes!"

"Full-time?"

I said, "Yes!"

She said, "It is going to be hard. You can't manage both full-time work and school. You would be setting yourself up for failure. Don't waste your time. Why don't you try part-time school? Also, we don't have the space for this month anyway, as all the classes are full."

She insisted that I couldn't do it because I would be too tired, and I couldn't manage to work full-time and keep up my studies at the same time. While I was listening to her, I couldn't help but remember fifteen years earlier when I was told I was garbage and that I could not go to high school in France. I had tears in my eyes, and my hands were shaking.

I said, "I have time to study. Please, I really want to, and it is necessary." I told her that I could study after work and on the weekends.

I added, "I know my English is not perfect. I am willing to work harder than most people. I really want to go to school."

At that point, I was so frustrated that I told her firmly that I would not move from that chair until she found a place for me. She picked up the phone and made a call. I didn't know what she was doing, but then she told me that I started the following Monday.

For two years, my schedule was 8:30 a.m. to 12:30 p.m. at school, and from 1:00 p.m. to 9:00 p.m. at work. I was having trouble getting to my job on time because it was forty-five minutes from my school. I explained the situation to my boss and asked if I could come fifteen minutes late every day for one year. I will never forget his answer. He said, "Yes! Not a problem. When you get better, we get better," and he continued to pay me even for those fifteen minutes I wasn't there. I had to be very organized to keep up with this schedule, so I had my lunch on the subway on my way to work and then studied from 10:00 p.m. until 1:00 or 2:00 a.m. each night.

I graduated from high school in June of 2017 in Toronto, Ontario, at the age of thirty-four. Who could imagine that one day I would have a high school diploma ... and in the English language!

Building the Muscle of Mindset

With an unnegotiable desire to go to school, I made the decision to make it happen, no matter the difficulty. My mind was made up and it was going to happen! And I was not going to take no for an answer! From that experience, I also understood that when we really want something, we do not see the difficulty. We don't even think about the difficulty. We wake up in the morning full of energy to face the possibilities (even with a lack of sleep!). As such, the formula that works for me is: "Determination + Desire + Choices + Action = Success." But this formula takes practice.

Once we take the first step of any dance, we have the potential to become a great dancer, even under stress. It doesn't matter where we are, what kind of life we have had, or who we are—we just must believe we can do it. Belief that we are capable of being the greatest version of ourselves is incredibly important. And belief that we can make a difference in the world, beginning with a small change in ourselves, is key. A small change in our way of thinking is how we begin to see changes all around us.

Oftentimes, lack of belief is what holds us back. Maybe we didn't get the education needed and we start to think we can't do it because of that. We literally sabotage ourselves by putting up barriers. Consequently, we stay stagnant in our fear. But we are the master of our own lives—we are the key. So, believe with your heart. Once you believe that anything is possible, you open the barriers you've placed in your mind. If you can imagine yourself on the top of the mountain with your flag of success, it's a sign that you are already a winner!

Remember this saying by Henry Ford: "Those who believe they can do something and those who believe they can't are both right."

It is all about building the muscle of your mindset. For example, when you are going to the gym, the more you work out, the stronger your muscles get. During the workout, you may feel pain and the next day you may be sore, but it's worth it. It is the same thing with mindset. Focusing on the things that work, the end results of your efforts (despite any pain) make you stronger.

I didn't realize that I was doing that as a child as well. It happened naturally for me, so I wasn't consciously aware of it, but I did it. Staying positive will inevitably make us stronger.

CHAPTER 14

ACCEPTANCE AND LOVE

Moving to Canada was a renaissance for me. There I was, adjusting to a new country once again and this time totally alone—not knowing anyone and not speaking the language. But it was a great opportunity to discover myself. It's like being a newborn baby that must learn everything and most importantly, yourself, from scratch. I learned a lot about my fears, my courage, my pain, and my joy.

I loved Toronto and its multiculturalism. When you walk the streets, you actually feel as if you are traveling around the world. You see the beautiful smiles of various people who have come there from many different countries. There are delicious ethnic foods that are as varied as the people who live there. And the real beauty of it all is that we live together in peace with a respect for each other's lives, cultures, and traditions.

As I went through the immigration process, I met some wonderful people who were there to help me. They welcomed me with open arms, as if I were automatically a part of their family. I was blessed to learn about their customs and enjoy their company on holidays and special occasions. The winters may be cold in Canada, but emotionally, I was very much warmed by the kindness and hospitality of my new extended family there.

I found this extremely helpful when dealing with another challenge—feeling as if I only had a temporary place there, with no destination in mind. Many people feel this when relocating to a new country before they obtain permanent residency. One can experience the feeling of going nowhere—feelings of having all their hopes and dreams put on hold. Some mornings, they may even wake up thinking, "Okay, this is it, I am going back now." But then, they remember they can't just give up. How would we reach our goals if each time we had a setback, we gave up? When your "why" is big enough, it keeps you going on your journey with strength, power, and determination.

More Acceptance and Less Judgment

We are all guilty at times of making judgments through the lens of our own experiences. We all need to be more aware of subconsciously acting in this way. We are all human, regardless of our skin color or language or the country in which we were born or raised. We all grew up with different cultures filled with music, dance, traditions, foods, and wonderful legacies. Those should be embraced, not frowned upon. This diversity is what makes life so colorful and wonderful. It would be extremely boring without it.

It doesn't matter to me who you are or where you're from. We all must try to better understand each other's differences and respect each other as we are. When we arrive with our suitcases, we settle in, and we just want to be accepted. We hope that others will understand our struggles, our fears, and our dreams, but we tend to forget that these same people also have their own struggles, fears, and dreams. They, like us, want to be understood. In the end, we all want the same things, but fear is what holds us back.

I believe that fear is the foundation of judgment. The dictionary states that fear is an emotion that causes anxiety or dread. In the subconscious, fear is there to protect us, but it also limits our capacity to improve ourselves. The presence of fear can create the worst scenarios in life. It can even stop us from getting up in the morning with a renewed sense of purpose to reach our dreams, fight for our rights, and stand up for others.

When acting out of the emotion of fear, we may automatically reject other people and cultures in order to protect our own, even if subconsciously. Once again, the intention behind fear could be good—it's to protect, but the other side perceives it in a different way. I believe that most of the time, all of our actions come from love and not fear. And if we take a step back, we can see that others' life journeys are not much different than our own. It doesn't matter who we are—immigrant or not. Culture, skin color, and religion do not matter—human is human. And if we actually take the time to exchange a few words or ideas, we can see that others are just like us. We all simply want to be accepted and loved. We are all one. We are all unique in our differences, and even in our similarities.

Through emigrating from Armenia to France and then to Canada, I found myself to be very fortunate. Some people take the opportunity to bridge cultures through travel, but not many choose to experience them long term. My experiences allowed me to choose my freedom as a woman, and not be imprisoned in a culture that I had been enveloped in since birth. This allowed me to decide which parts of each culture I wanted to include in my life, and which to let go of. From my vantage point, I noticed that not everything we learn in our culture brings us happiness. Consequently, I began to live my life in harmony with all that I had and continued to experience.

I feel that each experience and situation that we have teaches us something. Therefore, no experience is wasted if we listen to it carefully to understand the language. We will then realize that each one is an opportunity to not only improve ourselves, but to be a gift to the world. Despite all the difficulties we may encounter in our life, when we move far away from our home to discover other cultures, people, and countries, in the end, it is all worth it. During my immigration adventures, I discovered that the other side of the world is truly dreaming of doing the same thing. What I also discovered was that in wanting to discover another world, we are discovering ourselves. I am convinced that when we discover who we are, we will understand that there is no difference between us and other people—we are all ONE!

I imagine that immigrants are like an old fruit tree when it is uprooted to be replanted in new soil. It needs time to re-establish its root system and bear fruit. But it also needs to be taken care of, pruned to remove the bad growth, and given plenty of sunshine and water to let it grow and flourish. I know from my experience that if only we would all listen without any judgment, we could create a peaceful world. Imagine what might happen if we would all take one minute to ask what amazing story is hiding behind the next beautiful smile we see?

Usually, when we meet a person, we begin to communicate and often find common ground with them. When we are on the same page, so to speak, we may find we share similar levels of awareness, education, or experiences, and are therefore vibrating on the same level. Naturally, we have built a foundation to create a friendship or partnership, and it has nothing to do with the country from which we come.

Our origins, religion, cultural traditions, and skin color have nothing to do with the creation of our relationship with another person. What is most important is the soul of the person. How many times have we not been able to get along with a person of our own race or culture, or been unable to find any common ground with them? It is more important that we make the effort to share our values with each other—that which can only be found inside. What would happen if we saw each other with the eyes of our heart, instead of the eyes of our head? What would happen if we brought love to those we meet?

By taking time to get to know someone who is different than you, you open a whole new world and are blessed with the diversity that they can bring to your life. If only we could stop judging and accept each other as we are. And best of all, we can evolve together.

Once again, it doesn't matter what happened in our past. That won't dictate our future. What does matter is where we are going from here and what choices we make for tomorrow. As Gandhi said, "Be the change you want to see in the world."

CHAPTER 15

FORGIVENESS

I left Armenia a couple decades ago, but I finally went back as a tourist in 2018. My mother went with me. The country was not the same, but neither was I. I wanted to find out where my father was, what he was doing, and if he was still drinking. But first, I needed to find out if he was still alive. We had had no contact with him or anyone from that side of the family for many years.

If he was alive, my plan was to buy him a bottle of vodka and some groceries as a sign that I accepted and loved him for who he was. I wanted him to know I cared. I knew I would be the closest family member he had left. I figured he likely considered alcohol as his only family and only solace, so I would buy it for him if that's what made him happy. This did not mean I condoned or validated his actions or him being an alcoholic. It meant that I could empathize with him, and I could try to understand his addiction and sickness as another human being—and as his daughter.

I asked Mom if she remembered the address of where he lived and if she wanted to come with me to find him. I also told her that I would understand if she didn't want to come. Without any hesitation, she told me she was absolutely coming. She told me that she was ready. She wanted to support me on my journey, and because the last time she saw him nearly twenty years prior, he was drunk and violent. So, my mom, aunt, and cousin all joined me.

On the way to the last known address for him, I experienced a tsunami of different emotions. I was happy that I might see my father after all those years (I was now a thirty-five-year-old woman) and at the same time, I realized that I didn't really know him or even remember what he looked like. I was confused, scared, and nervous, but from the bottom of my heart, I knew I wanted to see him. When we arrived, excitement outweighed all the other emotions. I walked quickly ahead of everyone, my heart beating out of my chest.

As we approached, Mom said, "This is the building. The apartment is on the fifth floor." We arrived at the entrance to the building, and sitting under the trees was an older lady, maybe seventy-five or eighty years old. Mom asked her, "Do you know if Mark is still living on the fifth floor?"

"Oh, my darling, the apartment was sold a couple years ago, and he is not living here anymore," she said. She added that she heard he had died but suggested we check with a woman who lived on the third floor who had lived there for many years. My excitement was immediately replaced with devastation. I guessed my chance to get to know my dad was gone, just like he was.

We knocked on the door, and an elderly lady answered quicker than you might expect. Mom recognized her but didn't let it show that she did. She asked, "Could you please tell us about Mark on the fifth floor? Is he still alive?"

She looked at me and Mom curiously. She then said, "I know he passed away about eight years ago, and the house was sold."

We asked if she knew how he had passed, and she said that she wasn't sure but had heard that he had passed away drunk on one of the most beautiful streets of Armenia, where he spent many nights. The old woman kept staring at us. We could tell she wanted to ask who we were and if we were family members, but she didn't dare to do so. I think she recognized Mom, and she kept looking at me. From the look on her face, I could tell that she was guessing who I was, because apparently, I look just like my father. But we left her in suspense and didn't say anything more. There was nothing more to say.

Since I know that my father has passed away and no one knows where his body is buried, each time I go to Armenia, I visit the cemetery where my grandparents are buried. When I put flowers on their graves, I place an extra bunch beside them, as if his body is there. I can still give flowers to my unhappy, unloved father. At least his soul can feel that he is now loved by his daughter.

Forgiveness

When I understood what real forgiveness was, my questions disappeared, and there was nothing left to forgive. I choose (again, so much of life is about our choices) to understand why he behaved the way he did. As Neale Donald Walsch says, "Understanding replaces forgiveness." It is difficult not knowing all the answers to something, but it's also okay. We must accept that sometimes there are no answers. What I found instead was that someone who is not aware of the love that they are capable of usually hasn't had it to recognize it in the first place. Many have only had rejection in their lives, and therefore can't give something they don't think they have to give. For example, I can't ask a homeless person sitting on the sidewalk for money. If I did, they are likely to answer that they can't because they don't have any.

Can anyone be angry with them simply because they didn't give you what they do not have? Of course, they can't. In that same way, I developed a love for a father that I didn't really know personally. I only knew the bad things he'd done and what family members said about him. I never said anything, but since I found my inner peace with him, I found my love for him—the love that was hiding deep in my heart under the mask of protection and fear. I finally accepted him as my father. He is my father, I love him, and I know he did the best that he could.

CHAPTER 16

LIFE EXPERIENCES AND THE POSSIBILITIES THEY UNCOVER

My life experiences have taught me to understand that we can change our lives if we truly want to. Sometimes it's hard to believe in yourself, particularly when your childhood was embedded in abuse, distrust, and unending fear. For longer than I can remember, I witnessed brutality, both on a personal level and on those I loved. But that doesn't mean it defined my future.

I understand the stigma that each slap and punch imprints on your body, and even worse, your mind, heart, and soul. Each time it happens, you feel yourself asking what *you* did to allow this to happen to you. You may even feel guilty for being alive, as if you don't really matter. There is no doubt that it stifles your growth as a human being by ripping away your confidence and self-esteem. Eventually, your love for yourself dissipates, and subconsciously, you close yourself off to love from others. It is simply a coping mechanism to try to protect yourself from being hurt again.

We fear that we are not good enough to be loved. But the fact is, all those thoughts and feelings are in our subconscious. We don't even realize that the thoughts we have about our experiences have shaped our reality to the point that we feel we can do nothing about it. I grew up with all these feelings as a result of the physical and psychological abuse I endured. With time, I understood that I am more than what my abusers did to me. In fact, I am much more than that.

Even if we were told we were no good as a child and even if we believed those horrible things for a time, when we can find our self-love once again, we can rise above it. So much of it comes down not to what happens to us, but to how we react to those things. It's about how we choose to view each circumstance and situation that creates the quality of our lives. My grandparents taught me to consciously choose to look for the good in any given situation, even if it seemed negative. They would tell me that there is always something good that can come out of what appears to be harmful or even tragic. They always believed that 'tomorrow will be a new day,' and we can 'make it a great day.'

I also grew up knowing all about difficult financial situations. It was often a struggle to have enough food. Most of my clothes were hand-me-downs from family or neighbors. The only time I got new clothes was each September for the new school year. I was told not to run in my new shoes because I had to wear them for a couple of years. Any new clothing was always bought a bit larger so that we could wear it as long as possible.

But my grandparents did it in a way that didn't make me feel weak or poor. Rather, I felt rich inside, as we shared whatever we had with each other. The sincerity, honesty, and love we had in our hearts was magic and gave us something more important than material things. All those experiences—all those moments—have given me incredible strength and courage because I choose to see the wonderful moments that life gives me and then use them to empower me even more.

The good news is that no matter where you are in your journey, you can change all those beliefs by working on yourself. It isn't easy, but the best things in life never are. In time, you will realize that you are perfect just the way you are, and you deserve to be loved, appreciated, and respected. Now, you are probably saying that you aren't perfect. And you would be right, because no one is. The perfect I am talking about is being the perfectly imperfect human that you are. It is embracing your faults and weaknesses as much as your assets and strengths.

Now that I am an adult, I've come to understand what real happiness is and what truly matters to me. I understand that it is not being ungrateful to say that I am looking for a better life. When I say 'better,' I mean more happiness, more love, and more peace. And while I am blessed to have them all, we can always make them bigger and better. I believe it is possible to have all those beautiful things. I also believe that it is important to know the difference between being happy and being satisfied. It's my understanding that happiness is a state of mind coming from inside of us, while satisfaction is some external circumstance that meets our wants or needs.

During the process of changing, you may be judged and criticized. In fact, you likely will be judged and criticized. People don't like change—for themselves or for others. It makes them question things and consider different perspectives, and that makes most people uncomfortable. Some people that you considered friends (or even family) may leave you or they may be the first to criticize you. As difficult as it is, try not to take it personally. They may not be in the same place. They may be shifting themselves. Either way, their energy is on a different level than yours, and that's okay. Those who love you unconditionally will always be there and understand that growth means change. Those are the ones you want to hold onto. It reminds me of Shakespeare, when he said, "All the world's a stage, and all the men and women merely players; they have their exits and their entrances." It's okay if it's time for their exits.

I believe that nothing happens in this life without a reason. Sometimes, it's for a period of time in order to share our gifts and learn from each other in any given moment. We help each other evolve before we move on. I am so grateful to the people who came into my life—family, friends, acquaintances, all those who have crossed my path and touched my life in some way. They have allowed me the opportunity to discover myself with their actions, their attitude, their love, and yes, even their anger.

Thanks to our experiences, we can all evolve and see the beauty of the life that has made us who we are. Each person in our life can bring out the best in us and give us the opportunity to learn and grow in our own evolution. What would life look like if we hadn't had someone to share our joys and sorrows?

Although some of my life experiences have been challenging, I've never really thought of myself as a victim. I think this is partly due to the culture in which I grew up. As a child, I witnessed a lot of domestic violence around me that was often seen as a 'normal' part of life. As such, even though I had an inner knowing that it wasn't right, I made a conscious choice to accept my past circumstances and look for the wonderful and happy times that I had in my childhood. Consequently, I chose to dwell on and appreciate the beauty in life. I chose to wear a smile on my face and hold a song in my heart. As Neale Donald Walsch says, "Be the light unto the darkness."

It's important that we understand that we can't go back to change our past, but we can change our future with the actions that we take each and every day. In order to know what our future holds, we may need to look at our present and ask the question, "Is this what I want for my future?" If the answer is yes, then everything is perfect as it is, but if the answer is no, then it is up to us and us alone to act on it and make the necessary changes.

We are the masters of our future and have the capacity to create it the way we want. Impossible doesn't exist. Each morning when we open our eyes, we have a new chance and a new opportunity to create a new life. Let us begin to live it. And always remember … love is the answer.

For me, I refuse to allow my past to break me. I hope that you do the same.

EPILOGUE

Isn't it interesting how life experiences can bring us to a place that we never thought we would be? Once we are on the other side of these experiences, it's like crossing over a bridge. That bridge is paved with each and every heartache, challenge, hug, laugh, and tear of our lives. They came together to forge the path that we needed to take to get to the other side. We often don't see it as it's happening—we're too caught up in the here and now. But when we look back, we can see it clearly.

As I continue my path in life, I used to wonder how I could describe the joy and happiness I have in my heart and the love of life I have inside me. But then I realized what I learned through all my experiences is that it all comes down to sharing. I can share these thoughts and feelings with others. I can bring them all to those who would like to receive them and help them find their own happiness, joy, and love. I can help them find the key to the treasure that is hidden deep inside. And I have started this message with this book and through my work as a life and personal development coach, and motivational speaker.

It is my privilege to share my story and to bring my mom's story to light to help other people find their own courage to make the changes they need to live happier and with peace. It is also my privilege to say, "You are not alone! You can do it! You are the key to your life!"

If we open our minds and ask ourselves, "If that were me, with that pain, with that hunger, with that helplessness, would I like someone to help me? Would I like someone to give me a piece of bread? Would I like someone to give me a hand?" The answer, of course, is yes. So, when we answer those questions with honesty, we won't hesitate to give a hand to the other person. And only in this way can we make a change in our world. And one thing that we can always give that costs us nothing is love. So, let's give love to each other freely.

"We cannot create a new future by holding onto the emotions of the past." —Dr. Joe Dispenza

Yesterday is gone, and every day is a new day, with new opportunities to decide how we want tomorrow to look. Let us ask this question before making any decision—*Is the emotion I am feeling about a situation or someone or even about myself coming from my past experience or from my new self?* The answer will clear your path.

Sometimes, we say that we are turning the page of the book of life and starting a new chapter. In my case, I can say that I did not turn the page, I just started a new book with a new life, a new me, and a new way of thinking. Life can only change if we write our own chapter from that new perspective. Of course, it's not easy, and sometimes it can be very difficult, but when we are motivated and have the will to change our life so that each day is better than the day before, it is possible.

Life is a beautiful book that allows our own unique stories to be told. And while we are the author, the universe is the pen, guiding our hand along the way. We can never know what it will have us write. All we can do is try to learn from the difficult parts and yes, even be grateful for them in the same way we are grateful for all the wonderful parts—the laughter, the happiness, the peace, and as always, the love.

THE POWER OF POETRY

The Magic of Winter

Winter is here to clean the darkness
Winter is here to bring the light
Snowflakes dance in the sky
Under the music of the wind

The whiteness covers the scars of the pain
The earth dressed in whiteness spreads the peace
Winter is here to bring the message of God
That life is here knocking on your door
For you to live it and spread love

Winter is here and life also
Winter is here, say yes to it
Say yes to life, yes to love
Say yes to pain, yes to darkness

Winter is here, to bring the light
And clean the darkness
Winter is here, open the door
And life also

—Tehminé Grigorian

The Power of Belief

Let us not wish or hope that prejudice will change
Let us not wish or hope that discrimination will change
Let us not wish or hope that racism will change
Let us not wish or hope that violence will change
Let us not go to bed at night with regrets
But let us act with peace and make it happen

Nothing happens without taking action
It must be more than a wish in the mind
Take responsibility for making it happen
Let us believe that we can do it together
Impossible does not exist if we are
Willing to go outside of the box
Everything worthwhile happens outside of it

Once we cross the border
We must believe and not give up
We have to believe that this is the
Beginning of our new life and not the end
Despite the difficulty

We have to learn how to smile and stay positive
We have to focus on good things and
Not the things that are not working
If we are focusing on the things that are not working
We can at least see that those experiences
That we are calling problems
Are there to show us the way and teach us something
We just need to understand the language of it

—Tehminé Grigorian

Happiness

Happiness is me, and you
Happiness is when you are just happy, without reason
without condition
without demand and expectation
Happy just because
Happiness is love
And love, the essence of our existence
Love, the reason for our existence

Love, the source
Love, the Happiness
Happiness is the freedom to follow the voice of your heart
Happiness is knowing who you are
Happiness is respect of own self and others
Happiness is a state of being
Happiness is the joy of loving others as you would love yourself
Happiness is being connected with your soul
Happiness is the feeling of the Love of your essence
Happiness is you!
Happiness is me!
Happiness is us!
Happiness is being all together!

—Tehminé Grigorian

Love

Love, four magical letters
Constitutes one magical word
One word that can change everything
One's life and destiny

Love can heal pain
Love can heal illness
Love can bring peace
Love can be given and received unconditionally

Love is the essence
The roots of everything
Love gives you wings to fly
Courage to believe in yourself
Faith to trust your future
Joy to laugh every day
Peace to share with the world

With the eyes of love, you look at the person
In that moment, the human part doesn't exist anymore
You only see a soul
A pure energy of divinity
You feel a true self
You feel the energy and essence of love
And you recognize yourself in this soul
You don't see this love with your mind
You feel it through the eyes of your own soul

In that moment, the mind loses its power of judgment
and the ego disappears

and you are just becoming Oneness
and your soul starts to communicate with the
language of love and says:

I want for you what you want for You

This is speaking the language of soul
Soul understands only one language
The language of Love
And when that communication is happening
together you become One
with that oneness you become God
And you shine in front of the darkness

Two strangers become One
And dance together under the music of love
Laugh together under the rain
Sleep together under the eyes of the stars
Shine together next to the sun

Love, four magical letters
One magical word
One magical feeling that can bring two
souls together and create oneness

We become each other
Together we become One
And it's called unconditional love

—Tehminé Grigorian

ABOUT THE AUTHOR

Tehminé Grigorian is a successful life coach, author, and motivational speaker. Through her own personal and professional experiences, she has learned many direct life lessons that made enormous impacts on how she lives each day. She discovered that far too many people have a negative view of themselves, feeling as if they are unworthy of love. After years of working through her own personal challenges and working closely with others to help them do the same, she has developed a coaching system based on self-discovery, reflection, and love.

It is her mission in life to help make a positive change in the lives of others by helping them find their purpose and the tools and resources they need to be more successful in their careers, personal lives, and future ambitions.

Your Past Can't Break You is Tehminé's first book. When she is not coaching others or writing, Tehminé loves theater acting, soccer, reading, traveling, and enjoying delicious foods from all over the world.

For more information about Tehmine Coaching:

https://tehminecoaching.com/
https://tehminecoaching.com/books/
Tehminecoaching@outlook.com
Instagram : @tehminecoaching
Facebook : Tehminecoaching

TehmineCoaching

Manufactured by Amazon.ca
Bolton, ON